♫ Mine All Mine Can Be Yours ♫

A Collection of Inspirational Messages,
Gospel Songs, Biblical Scriptures,
Poetry and Prayers
To Bring You Closer to
The Love of our Lord Jesus Christ

By
Charles A. Jones

Tampa, Florida

Then Peter opened *his* mouth,
And said, of a truth I perceive that
God is no respecter of persons
Acts 10:34

authorHOUSE®

Published by AuthorHouse   07/07/2014

ISBN: 978-1-4208-6172-3 (sc)

Library of Congress Control Number: 2005905243

This book is printed on acid-free paper.

Cover concept by Author
Back cover written by Author

Dictionary terms from Oxford and
Webster Dictionary – used by permission

All Scripture quotations marked KJV are from
the Holy Bible, King James Version
other scriptures, quoted from the Living Holy Bible kjv

Unless otherwise noted, all scripture quotations are
from the Holy Bible

Used by Permission

Please send all correspondence to:
Freedom of True Word Production c/o
Attn: Charles Jones
Post Office Box 310871
Tampa, FL 33680-0871
or email cjones_mark1124@yahoo.com

God has not fogotten you, hold
your head up high and be true
to Him and He'll open doors...

This lyric above was quoted by
Bishop Walter L. Hawkins from
the Love Alive II Live Recording
© 1978 Light records

Mine All Mine / Can Be Yours

A Collection of Inspirational Messages, -
Gospel Songs, Biblical Scriptures,
Poetry and Prayers
To Bring You Closer to
The Love of our Lord Jesus Christ

Messenger by Charles Jones
21st century

but they that wait upon the Lord
shall renew their strength; They shall
mount up with wings as eagles; and
they shall walk, and not faint.
Isaiah 40:31

Charles Jones

TABLE OF CONTENTS

MINE ALL MINE / CAN BE YOURS

What is the source of this project?

I am certain this project of mine "Mine All Mine / Can Be Yours: will make an example for all walks of life. Whether you are pursuing a career, a goal or just living day by day, the purpose of this project is the same. I suggest that you love, live and pursue your life with the love of the Lord Jesus Christ.

Remember this, God sent his only begotten Son to die for our habits in life; that we can arrive through the blood he shed on the hills of Calvary. So, my friend, whatever you think you know or don't know, try Him because of that.

I tried Him and have realized that He is real, and God is real. I know and you know that we can't live without Him. Whether you like it or not, you can't. So, stop faking God and yourself.

Be honest in what you do. Remember always, for your sake, don't block Him out of your life. Okay?

Remember this also, God has not forgotten you, hold your head up high and be true to Him and He'll open doors to your heart. We are human beings and there is such a thing as trying with God's help always whether it's right or wrong. He won't let you fall any further then your bending your knees to pray, my child. He'll understand.

Jesus Christ was a man of goodness; He was sent to mend examples of our sin sick souls. So behave and have faith. Let Jesus Christ rest within your heart, and trust and obey His commandments.

For this is the will of God Almighty above all things. **Amen.**

Thank you, Jesus, for this message of acknowledgment.
January 24, 1989

As long as I am in the world,
I am the light of the world.
John 9:5

About the Author

October 25, 1999

About the Author
CHARLES' STORY

Charles Jones was born in Tampa, Florida, 1966, resided in Hillsborough County. He attended local elementary and graduated high school in 1986 and attended a community college in Tampa Bay Area. He was raised and attended a local traditional Baptist Church, called Mount Tabor Missionary Baptist Church where he was baptized at a young age. "*That's where all of my soul and the love of gospel music came from,*" *I will confessed honestly.* His father was a seaman laborer and his mother was a homemaker and pianist. I was the fourth of four children of Charley and Annie Jones. I am not writing this story for you to feel pity for me, but to listen and try to understand my view point as a young boy growing up was quite a challenged for me to do.

It started when I was born, an 8 pound and 11 ounce bouncing boy coming home from the hospital for everyone to adore. While I was growing up, I was pampered. My older sister, Paula, babysat with me every Wednesday night while my mother, Annie (everyone called her Mamma Ann), attended choir rehearsal at 7:30p.m.I would sit home with my sister and listen to her albums. That always put me to sleep. My sister took good care of my younger sister, Maude and me.

My mother said that at the age of two, I was always singing, no matter what the situation. Singing kept me busy and out of trouble. It kept my attitude positive and it kept the negative thoughts about people out of my mind.

Growing up in the Tampa Bay Project neighborhood was difficult in many ways. The difficult part was the neighborhood children, who would sometimes call me names, and my family. My mother would always take me to church to participate in church activities. I was an introverted child, but I always enjoyed the singing. My sister, Paula, was always working. She is the eldest and appeared to be the smartest of the group, but also was very fussy and very critical, at times. Though I admire her tenacity.

My brother, Urschell is the comedian in the family. He kept us laughing all the time with funny skits. I really love my brother, but I never felt in the same category as he, thus making it hard for me to look up to him. I thought this might be attributed to the vast age difference between us.

My younger sister, Maude, was puny until she grew older and attractive to the older boys. Maude and I got along very well. She would always do my homework for me. Thanks, Maude, for taking care of that problem.

My mother had her children starting in her early twenties. She had us spaced a part which was considerably harmless. Even though I was the baby, I did not always get my way. God knows, I tried. I've kindled my way through childhood. Everyone would always tell my mother or me how precious or cute I was. They would never tell me that I was bright. I guess they did not know this. It took time for me to realize this, too.

I was always busy singing my songs. It was special to me to sing on the front porch. People would pass by, and then stop to listen to see if they could understand what I was singing. I would sing off key a lot. I was marking my Lord Jesus' words. I knew what I was singing was true, and hoped that those who understood the words perceived the same as I.

Growing up in the Belmont Height Projects area, I would play with the kids that I could handle and rule. I always wanted to be the leader of the bunch. I wanted things to go my way because Charles knew best. And things always did go my way. I was very ungrateful growing up. My mother told me that, but I never knew what the word ungrateful meant until now.

Therefore, now it scares the heck out of me because I've been told I was so ungrateful and inconsistent so much until I accepted this as a weapon through the years. Then ignoring became my main source in my life when unfortunate remarks were told to me from my family and friends that God was watching over me. Even though I did not know him or it never was inspired in me. I just knew him by imitative behavior. Who was I thinking that I was fooling God? He knows every situation you go through. So, I'm going to wait for the Lord.

Charles' Story

Train up a child in the way he should go: and
When he is old, he will not depart from it.
Proverbs 22 : 6

ASSURANCE

These things I have written to you who believe in the
name of the Son of God, that you may know that you
have eternal life, and that you may continue to believe
in the name of the Son of God

1 John 5:13 KJV

For I am persuaded that neither death nor life, nor angels
nor principalities nor powers, nor things present nor
things to come, nor height nor depth, nor any other
created thing, shall be able to separate us from the love
of God Which is Christ Jesus our Lord

Romans 8:38-39 kjv

NEW BEGINNING

Let go. Clean the slate and gain courage for a fresh start
with the fruity florals in New Beginning. Daring starts
from within. You have a safe passage to grow beyond
your self-imposed limitations. Inside, prana, your life
force energy burns strongly. If you listen, you'll discover
what your soul is trying to tell you. Imagine yourself
soaring like an eagle high above mundane daily details.
Suddenly, your soul takes flight. As you soar, you can
finally see the larger landscape around you. It's full of
new possibilities. Things are clearer. Be alert to what is
beginning to awaken in you.

Unknown-

The Body Is The Temple Of God

To those who wanted to be saved by
the holy spirit of God, we need to be more
submissive, brethren, by the mercies
of God, that ye present your bodies
a living sacrifice, holy, acceptable
unto God. And be not conformed to
this world: but be ye transformed
by the renewing of your mind, that
ye may prove what is that
good, and acceptable, and perfect,
will of God. Romans 12:1-2

the body is the temple of God
created for protection over our soul
we live temporarily in our body, so we
should keep and maintain an even
balanced of health and nourishment,
Let it dwelled within by the blood of Jesus

I beseech you therefore, be obedient
and serve the Lord with praise and
song, and let the trumpet sound
Rejoicing, Rejoicing, Rejoicing more rejoiced
Let heaven ring forevermore in the
sanctuary unto God in Jesus Name. Amen.

-Charles Jones

© 2005 *The Body Is The Temple Of God* by Charles Jones

❧PRAISE GOD FOR THIS DELIVERANCE❧

weeping may endure for a night, but joy *cometh* in the morning

Psalm 30:5

This book was created and researched, before I knew that
I was writing a book to format for published or reading. I chose the title:
Mine, All Mine and could not let it go from my hand, for over seventeen
years. In mind I knew it would benefit others and me in the future.
Therefore, through the experienced of my sins; I had to keep writing
poetry and prayers for comfort. As, I continue to write I dealt in this tangled of immoral
lifestyle behavior, indulging in high maintenance, alcohol, drugs and suffer
emotional depression.
Despite my shortcomings and fallen,
God has not given up on me.
His favor has given me faith and perseverance.
To sow a seed in fertile ground rooted so deep, that as a child I would grow up and be able
to weather the raging storm in my adulthood. Deliverance is a process in the wailing and
praying in the Spirit of God, through the son that was given to the world as a redeemer and
deliverer. What a blessing to have a mother who
believed in steering her children to church. Though, I never gave up I never let those lustful
behavior seal me. I am a man after God's on heart, before I was
born God had a plan for me. God has anointed me and healing began and deliverance came
like a strong tower in my weakest hour." I Surrender All" *I PRAISED YOU ADONAI*
I OWE YOU MY LIFE JEHOVAH-ROHI
"The Lord is my Sheperd"
Psalm 23

from the author

Responsibility is a funny thing:
The more we try to
avoid it, the more we
run up against it.
But when shoulder
it squarely,
it strengthens us
and becomes the
cornerstone of our
character and the
foundation that
supports so many
other good qualities.

Unknown-

But they that wait upon the Lord
shall renew their strength; They shall
mount up with wings as eagles; they
shall run and not be weary; and
they shall walk, and not faint.

Isaiah 40:31 kjv

Mine All Mine   Can Be Yours

Charles Jones

Praise God For What You Know

And my tongue shall speak of thy righteousness *and* of thy praise all the day long
Psalm 35:28

In your daily walk with the Lord - and all that you know in your heart
Keep on pressing on toward the mark - and don't let interruption in your mind;
Clutter your mind with gossip and back biting - but with the -Gospel of Jesus Christ
Praise Him for what you know- and all the love which flows plentifully from above.
Let the word of God touch your knowledge
To be developed into wisdom of courage.
That you might put away the old things
That will make way for the new things to come
Go ahead for what you know and Praise Him
Praise God for what you know…
Your walk will not be easy. Therefore, it will be times
the enemy will put your mind and body to the test, as you walked mindfully in the wilderness
He will try to make your life a living hell
He will make you want to turn your back on God
He will make some things appear as if God
blessed you with them - just remember what the devil meant
For your bad - God will turn around for your good
In your situation wherein you had no idea that you could survive this depth of
mockery; contemptuous behavior act in action. Steadfast and-
Go ahead for what you know and praise God with all
you know and do in the name of Jesus Christ our Savior
Keep on praising God for what you know…
And don't you give up!
He is a mighty God to serve night and day in the spirit
Let your praise validate your salvation
that you are worthy to Praise God even in your mess,
Look to Jesus even if it's not your fault or if it is your fault.
Remember for what you know and don't know-
God will provide like He said, he would.
He is Jehovah jireh our provider - Genesis 22:8

Go ahead and Praise Him as you cry out with a loud shout!

© 2005 Praise God For What You Know- by Charles Jones-

xx

The Bible kjv

And that from childhood you have known the Holy Scriptures, which are able to make you wise for salvation through faith which is in Christ Jesus. All Scripture is given by inspiration of God, and is profitable for doctrine, for reproof, for correction, for instruction in righteousness.

2 Timothy 3:15-16 kjv

Hello! Generations

Study your Bible daily and see what you can develop;
than pass it down from generation to generation...

Charles

Hello! Generations, here we are at last...
It may come as a surprise that we meet again...
To a stand still in holy vision that the
generation before you instilled.
Don't leave us behind;
include us in your endeavors and future.
You know we will support your goals.
We must work together as a team.
If there are some generational curses
we must solve them.
We must get on our knees and pray without ceasing
in a dimensional place where God is concerned.
That will be where God will give you a purpose
and a goal {Acts} to begin your future in
the land where your sons and daughters will
also know their purpose and goals.
There are four things they will need on their journey:
spiritual needs...emotional and mental needs...
physical needs...also material needs
to be utilized in the earthly realm.
These all will be met according to His riches and glory
that we are all called according to His purpose.
We must wait on the Lord.
Generations, as you follow your dreams and purpose,
take a piece of us with you so when you say to your children after dinner
"Let me pass down to generation to generation to come"
that you might not forget what you've learn firsthand
and that no man can take away because it is from the heart and soul.
You see how we are so spiritually blessed...to have had
grandparents and parents who cared enough to show us
the right way to righteousness in Jesus' name. Praise God. Amen.

© 2005 Hello! Generations by Charles Jones

PREFACE

REMEMBER THIS

To everyone who desires to strive through the Lord Jesus Christ, to be the very best that he or she can be. May God bless you in every way.

"Remembering without ceasing your work of faith, and labor of love, and patience of hope in our Lord Jesus Christ, and in the sight of God and our Father."

I Thessalonians 1:3

Remember God has not forgotten you; remember this, lift Him up for He will see you through, my friend.

Love,

Charles

A DEDICATION

This entire project is
Dedicated to my Father
Charley Jones
aka
(Uncle Charley)
I Love You, Dad.
you sowed a good seed...

The Eternal Goodness

I know not what the future hath
of marvel or surprise,
assured alone that life and death
His mercy underlies.

And if my heart and flesh are weak
To bear an untried pain,
The bruised reed He will not break,
But strengthen and sustain.

And so, beside the silent sea,
I wait the muffled oar;
No harm from Him can come to me to me
On ocean or on shore.

I know not where His islands lift
Their fronded palms in air;
I only know I cannot drift
Beyond His love and care.

J. G Whittier

Honor thy father and thy mother, as the Lord thy God hath commanded thee; that thy days may be prolonged, and that it may go well with thee, in the land which the Lord thy God giveth thee.
DEUTERONOMY 5:16

Meanin' of What? A Message

Message (mes-ij) *n*. 1. a spoken or written communication. 2. the inspired moral or social teaching of a prophet or writer etc., *a film or book with a message; get the message (informal) to understand what is meant or implied Oxford dictionary*

ANNIE, MOTHER WHO CARES

Mother who cares and understands.
Mother who lives to live again in Christ.

To a special wonderful lady who
I've gotten to love and know better than better.

She is my mother, Annie, who
I love dearly with my heart of the Lord.

Just speaking and writing in words
cannot express my love of my mother...

Praying for her and without ceasing
from my heart is more than best of love...

So,

I love you, mother always
through what ever may come between us..

With,

The love of God, no one can separate
us as we are

Because we love Jesus...
I love you, mother
May God bless you in every way.

Son,
Charles Jones

For thou hast possessed my reins: thou hast
covered me in my mother's womb.
Psalm 139:13

ACKNOWLEDGEMENTS

I have happily discovered firsthand, to never underestimate or overestimate anyone's abilities in this life. If God has allowed that special being to work for him, He can do most anything. "God's Will." There is no limitation in life when you have Jesus as a friend. And when you cooperate with Jesus, I am sure you can do all things; for all things are possible in Him. Remember, everywhere you go, have God first in your life for it's true, my friend. So, I would like to thank God, my teacher for His continuing love that revolves around me. Thank you Lord, for your endless grace and perseverance.

"Grace be with all them that love our Lord, Jesus Christ in sincerity. Amen." -Scripture-

Ephesians 6:24

INTRODUCTION

When you feel your faith is weak, let this be a recommendation to you:

"Now faith is the substance of things hoped for, the evidence of things not seen.
For by it the elders obtained a good report.
Through faith we understand that the world were framed by the word of God,
So that things which are seen were not made of things which do appear.
But without faith, it is impossible to please him; for he that cometh to God must believe that he is, and that he is a rewarder of them that diligently seek him."

Hebrews 11:2, 3, 6

"The Lord hath done great things for us; whereof we are glad."

Psalms 126:3

"Praise ye the Lord. Praise the Lord, O my soul.
While I live, will I praise the Lord.
I will sing praise unto my God while I have any being."

Psalms 146:2

Chapter 1
WORDS
OF A
SIMPLE
PLAN

A PRAYER TO GOD [1]

Dear Lord, I feel deprived in my soul. Please help me to overcome the agonizing pain that I have suffered in life.

To those who do not care, show them the light and make their fellowship bright through Your amplified power among all creeds, the afflicted, and all nationalities.

I pray on and on in Your name, Lord, asking forgiveness by confession, that my soul may be purified and my vision may be focused on the light of Your spirit. Lord, also, freshen my tongue so that I may speak of Your name wisely. Speak to me, Lord, in my ear so that I may perceive sounds and heed every command of Your precious voice.

All this I ask in the name of Thy son, Jesus. Amen.

Charles Jones

Continue in prayer, and watch in the same
with thanksgiving.
Colossian 4:2

WORDS
OF A
SIMPLE
PLAN
II

The Lord is my strength and song, and is become my salvation.

Psalms 118:14

The entrance of your words give light; it gives understanding to the simple

Psalms 119:130

Blessed be God, even the Father of our Lord Jesus Christ, the Father mercies, and theGod
of all comfort; who comforteth us in all our tribulation, that we may be able to comfort
them which are in any trouble, by the comfort wherewith we ourselves are comforted of God.
II Corinthians 1:3-4

TRUE LOVE

True Love True Love

True Love

(True Love)

Oooh True Love is God

Who can love you forever

No one can love you better like

the way My God can because

His love is so meaningful and plentiful

When you're down and low in your life

And you feel no one cares

Jesus is right there to hold your hand

to comfort and hold you (yes)

If you open your heart to God

"Surely goodness and mercy shall

follow you all the (Days) of your (life)"

Ooooh (yes)

True Love True Love

True Love

(True Love) is God of peace within your heart

(True Love) is God of joy nothing but pure joy.

(True Love) is God Our Heavenly Father Above.

Intermission:
a moment
of silence
in prayer...

Ask, and it will be given to you; seek, and you will find; knock, and it will be opened to you

St Matthew 7:7 kjv

PRAISE GOD

Oh come, let us sing unto the Lord.

Let us make a joyful noise to the rock of our salvation...

Let us come before his presence with Thanksgiving,

and make a joyful noise unto him with psalms...

Oh come, let us worship and bow down.

Let us kneel before the Lord Our Maker.

For the Lord is a Great God, and a

Great King above all gods...

For He is Our God,

and we are the people of his pasture,

and the sheep of his hand...

Harden not your heart, as in the provocation,

and in the day of temptation in the wilderness

In His Hand are the deep places of

the earth, the strength of the hills and mountains...

Oh praise His name in the most high...

Psalms 95: You are weary.

YOUR NAME

Lord, I stand in the promise
of your name...

I pledge in my heart I'll never
call out your sweet name
in vain no, no Lord

I will be a impious fool not to accept
you as my guide through this
wicked land...

So I need you Father, I need
your hand (yes, I do)

Oh How I Love to call your name
Your name is the answer to
all mankind, and the living
waters that flow in our hearts and
veins

Oh how I love your name. It's
sweet as the cherry tree...
Your name Your name
Oooh yes, your name

SUCCEED

No matter how hard we try there's
always someone out there to put
you down – (down) – (down)
But with the help of God, Our Lord
We will (succeed) these (trial)

No matter who we are there's
always someone there who
doesn't like the color of our skin
Whether we're (red) (yellow) (black)
    or (white)
But with the help of God, Our Lord
we will (succeed) these (trial)

We all have a purpose and goal
in our minds and hearts that will
carry us onto the promised land
Remember our trust lies in God
And with that determined we will (succeed)
       life as it stands...
       (We will succeed)
         Solo-
       (Repeat to fade)

LOOK DOWN

Spiritually in prayer

Dear God, Our Father
Please Look Down
and see my people through
(Oooh...Please Lord)
Lord, make us in Thy
own way to see you through
on Judgment Day...
God, we need you to look
down on us. Because it's
been said, Your love
touches in so many
ways of every precious day
(Oooh...Everyday)
Look down Lord we
need your love and peace
Look down and keep us
from the dust of sin
I know (we will win)
Give us the blessings we
need to glorify your name
Give us the hope we need
to endure the trust you give, Dear Lord
God, we thank you
(thank you) within our
hearts for (Jesus Christ) Our Savior...

Chorus:

Look down Look down
and make a way
Look down Look down
and make a way
Somehow Someway
Someday
Please Lord, Look down
Look down, Please Lord
Please Look down
Look down Please
Lord.
Amen.

Praying always with all prayer and supplication in the
Spirit, and watching thereunto with all perseverance and
And supplication for all saints
Ephesians 6:18

HERE I AM! SEND ME.

The world seems to be departing from God
Is it going down, down, down, down, down hill

You see we need someone to remove this world
stricken by sin (I know we can win)
We need someone to teach to our
children. They need to know that God
loves them in so many ways

Will anyone say, "Here I am! Send me
(Repeat 2 twice)
Here I am! Send me

"I'll go, I'll go, I'll go," said, A voice
and spread God's holy word in prayer

Can anyone tell me
who wants to be more like Isaiah
(Tell me who)

When God spoke from His lips
He said, "Whom shall I send, and will
go for us And Isaiah replied: "Here
I am! Send me" God then commanded:
"Go, and you must say to these people
Hear again and again.

If they don't believe in God's word
keep trying, keep preaching, keep serving

Well Isaiah said, "Lord, Lord. How
long (How long) will it take the people
to understand your word?" And he answered,
"Until the cities are wasted without
inhabitant, and the houses without man,
and the land be utterly desolate.

Here I am! Send me
Send me Lord Please send me

Here I am! Send me
Send me Lord Please send me

GOD IS THE PERFECT ONE
IN MY LIFE

Well, as you know,
I've been searching for that someone,
perfect someone in my life

Struggling and striving seemed to get me
down and nowhere

God is God is God is (The perfect one)

You see I was looking in the
wrong place at the wrong time
and got me nowhere

God is God is God is (The perfect one in my life)

Well, I said, "Let me kneel down
and pray cause praying can do
some good," I said, "Lord; Lord;
please lift me up, please Lord,
remove these heavy burdens of mine
I carry in my heart."

God is the perfect one in my life
God is the perfect one in my life

Something came over me like
a shower of God's love,
I felt the Holy Spirit movin'
about in my soul (Yes, I did)

Perfect one take control (control)
Please take control of my life
(of my life)

I knew He heard my prayer
than I knew I have found that

God is the perfect one in my life
Yes I did, He is the perfect one
in my life

No man hath seen God at any time. If we love
one another, God dwelleth in us, and his love
is perfected in us.
I john 4:12

11

Prayer scripture to the wise

Until now you have asked nothing in My name.
Ask, and you will receive, that your joy may be full.
John 16:24 kjv

EVERYBODY OUGHT TO PRAISE GOD

Everybody ought to praise God
Everybody ought to praise God
Everybody ought to praise God
Everybody ought to praise God

Praise His Holy name
Praise His Holy name

Everybody ought to praise God
Everybody ought to praise God
Everybody ought to praise God
Everybody ought to praise God

Praise His Holy name
Praise His Holy name

Praise Him in the morning
Praise Him in the noonday
Praise Him in the evening
Praise Him in the night

Praise His Holy name
Praise His Holy name

Why don't you praise God
   for your health?
Why don't you praise God
   for your life?
Why don't you praise God
   for the best?
Why don't you praise God
   FOR THE LIGHT?
Praise His Holy name
Praise His Holy name

God is worthy,
Yes, He's worthy of Praises

Praise His Holy name
Praise His Holy name

For with thee is the fountain of life:in thy
light shall we see light.
Psalms 36:9

13

SOUND OF JESUS

Talk to me, oh Lord
Talk to me, oh, oh Lord
Talk to me, oh, oh, oh Lord...(Talk to me)
Umm umm umm Oh so - so sweet (my, my)
Talk to me, oh Lord
Talk to me, oh, oh Lord
Talk to me, oh, oh, oh Lord...(Oh talk to me)
                                        (Oh Lord)

When you think you're alone
Jesus is right there to call your own
There is nothing like the sound of Jesus Christ
Voice, echoing in the wind
And you know, there is no end of tomorrows
Suffer (suffer) no sorrows (sorrows)

(The sound of Jesus) is pleasing (pleasing to the ear)
(the sound of Jesus) is healing (healing have no fear)

Talk to me, oh Lord
Talk to me, oh, oh Lord
Talk to me, oh, oh, oh Lord...(Oh talk to me oh Lord)
(The sound of Jesus), is really real (really real)
(The sound of Jesus), is for kneeling (for kneeling)
(Down to pray, to lead you to the right
path in life) (His sweet path in life)

(The sound of Jesus), is to meditate
(meditate and have faith)
(The sound of Jesus), is not to procrastinate
(Don't procrastinate and be unsaved)

Sound of Jesus is so very, very sweet
Taste and you will see (for yourself)
He touches also the hearing impaired
He simmered down like a glaze, on a
fruited pair, (oh yes), (yes, He is the fruit of life)
(more)

Sound of Jesus, oh sweet sound
Sound of Jesus, oh talk to me
Oh, sound of Jesus, oh, hear the sound
    of Jesus

Oh, sound of Jesus (need to hear)
    sweet God's word talking to me
Oh, sound of Jesus (need to feel)
    you in my body and soul
Please! Oh Lord, take control of my life
(I don't want to lose this fight)

Sound of Jesus
       Come to me
Sound of Jesus
       need to hear
Sound of Jesus
       in my ear
(The) Sound of Jesus (sound)
       like music
Sound of Jesus (is)
       really moving
       in my soul

Jesus, I need your sweet sound
Jesus, don't leave me now
(He said, "He wouldn't ever leave
us, never, never leave us.")

For we are made partakers of Christ, if we hold the beginning of our confidence
steadfast unto the end; while it is said, Today if ye will hear his voice, harden not your hearts.
Hebrews 3:14-15

15

NOBODY CAN'T

Expressively with warm vigor   Words by Charles Jones

Choir: (three times)

Nobody can't, Nobody can't
Nobody can't turn me around
from happiness

Nobody can't, nobody can't
Nobody can't turn me around
from happiness

God gives me joy deep down inside
And He said, "He will abide in me."

Nobody can't, nobody can't
Nobody can't turn me around
from happiness

Nobody can't, nobody can't
Nobody can't turn me around
from happiness

God gives me peace deep down inside
And He said, "He shall live in
me eternally."

(Don't you know that)
Love comes from God
In Him you can arrive
Joy comes from God
so plentiful that He is so wonderful
Peace comes from God
He gives it everyday. No one can
take it away
Love, Joy, Peace, all from
God, so be happy Dear One

So remember
Nobody can't, nobody can't
Nobody can't turn you
around from happiness

BE BLESSED AND RECEIVE

When it seems all hope is gone
It's only in your mind child
Love will find a way to bring it back
Make it your own, (child)
Time and time again, fears and doubts
lingers over our head, (look up to Jesus)
Fears and doubts will be carried out
Be blessed and receive
Be blessed and receive (God's blessings),
And never doubt in His word
Believe and be blessed and receive
God's Holy Tower (He'll give you power)
Believe and be blessed and receive
God's Holy Tower (wash with it every hour)

Believe and be blessed and receive
Believe and be blessed and receive
Believe and be blessed and receive
Believe and be blessed and receive (God's blessing)
It belongs to you who ever trust and obey
And let his word abide in you
For He will make a way
Somehow, somewhere
My child, my dear child

WHY COMPLAIN?

Words by Charles Jones

Sometimes life can be so cruel
Everyone around you tries to rule
Sometime you never see the light of day
Clouds in the sky will surely make a way

What I wondered why we want so much?
And all we do is make a fuss
Over something we cannot control at time
(If only, If only we stick and bind together)
(In time, day by day, if we control ourselves)
In any kind of weather (we can have
    the best of things) in life, in life!
Why do we complain, (complain) about
    the troubles we face in life
when you know they will just double?

Why complain? God is on the way
Why complain? God will make a way
Why complain? May your heart be not dismayed
Why complain? In life have faith (have faith)

Why do we complain about the
    pains we (suffer) in life when we have
Jesus (Jesus) Jesus Christ?

There is a solution to everyone's problems
Surely, surely we live, we will find an
    answer (Lord above...)

Why complain, when you have
    your health (your health)?
Why complain, when you're not
    on your deathbed (deathbed) (your deathbed)?

So why complain, (If you have Jesus)?
Oh, just say a prayer (prayer) (a prayer)
God will amend your needs
    (your needs) and our ways   Amen

LOVE NEVER FAIL

Inspired by Romans 8
Lyrics by Charles Jones

Love never fail
Love never fail
Love never fail...(me never)

Heartaches and pain (comes and goes)
   (comes)
Heartaches and pain (comes and goes)
   (goes)
There is no need of falling apart
Love will never fail (because) God never fails
Just have faith
For he will make a way

When you're hurt and torn
   of a broken heart
And feel someone is pulling
   you apart
Love will never fail
Love will never fail (you never) (you betcha)
Time will only tell
   When you need some help
Love will never fail

Love will never fail
You pray for that love above (above)
You pray for that hope (for tomorrow)
Love will never fail
Love will never fail
Love will never fail

	Love	Never	Fail	
Love		Will	Never	Fail
	Love	Never	Fail	
	hope we need...			
	Love	Never	Fail	
Love		Will	Never	Fail
	Love	Never	Fail	
	time we need...			
Love		Will	Never	Fail
	Love	Never	Fail	

IF YOU CARE FOR SOMEONE

Children, It's time to grow up!
    we need to give help to
    someone who is (less fortunate)
        (fortunate)

Children, It's time to get right!
    and bring together in perfect harmony...
        (harmony)

Chorus:

If you care for someone
    give them a hand...A (hand)
If you care for that someone
    make that stand...(stand)

REPEAT CHORUS

If you care for someone
    in need...(in need), it will relieve
        some pain
If you care for that someone's
    love...(love) everlasting love (love)

I believe...(every good and perfect)
Good and perfect gift comes from
    God. I believe one of God's gifts
    towards men is to help your fellow
    man when he's down to his last
        And you will be blessed

Children, someone is
    in need
        make it your time
Children, when someone is
    in need of prayer
    find time...

Oh, oh, oh, oh children
If you care for someone
    (give your time)
Oh, oh children
If you care for someone
    (make it your own time)
    to help someone in need   Ad lib

Every good gift and every perfect gift is
from above
James 1:17

I WILL TRUST IN THEE

Transcribed by Charles Jones

In God I will praise His word
In God I have put my trust in Him
I will not fear what flesh can do
           unto me
In God I will praise His word
In God I have put all my trust in the
           Father
I will not be afraid what man
           can do unto me

When every day my enemies wrest
           against my words
And with all their thoughts are against
           me for evil
I know the Lord will deliver
           my feet from falling
So that I may walk before God
           in the light of the living?
And my soul shall be forgiven
      (oh yes)

     I will trust in Thee
Oh yes, I will trust in Thee
     I will trust in Thee
Oh yes, I will trust in Thee
     I will trust in Thee
Oh yes, I will trust in Thee
       Oh yes, I will put
           all my trust in Thee

The lord is my rock, and my fortress, and my deliverer; my God,
My strength, in whom I will trust; my buckler, and the horn of my
Salvation, and my high tower.
Psalms 18: 2

CHANGING MY LIFE

Words by Charles Jones

Walking this life alone can be very hard
Everything around you seems oh so far away
We can very our lives in a positive way
    and make it last out through God's pathway

Walking this life alone can be rough
Everything around you can be oh so tough
    make it yours For Jesus is enough

To change your life for the better
To change your life can't be any sadder
Than what they are
Make that change for who you are

There was a time when I just wanted
    to die and throw my life away
      Oh, so sad!
There was a time when I just wanted
    to fly away to make my life
      a better place
I want to be able to endured the
    changeable life God has for me
No matter how hard it gets trials made
    great or small
I don't want to fall, Lord

Someday I'll take my wings
    and flop my feathers
And fly beyond the sky
And fly real high
In harmony and live forevermore
    eternity
(more)

Changing your life
    can or will be the best thing
    that could ever happen to anyone
    I know there is best yet to come

Changing my life (will)
    bring on a brighter day ahead
In time if I want it
    it can be mine
I used to think it was all
    in the mind
    changing my life
Something tells me everything
    is gonna be fine

I would say, "Oh what a great day for this change."
Telling me right from wrong making
    me oh so strong

Bridge:

Changing my life
    for the better
Changing my life
    for naturally
Changing my life
    in any kind of weather
Changing my life
    in perfect harmony
Changing my life (my life)
    will be the best yet to come
I know I'm gonna survive through
    this sad, sad, sad, sad fight

I thank you, Lord above, for your love

And be renewed in the spirit of your mind;
and that ye put on the new man, which
after is created in righteousness and true holiness
Ephesians 4: 23-24

DON'T LEAVE ME THIS WAY

I have been seeking here and there
I can't find my way
I have been seeking right from wrong
I can't seem to go on, God

Don't leave me this way
Oh Lord, don't leave me this way...
I need you night and day
Seems like times are tough and long
Lord, I want to be strong

Don't (don't) leave (leave) me (me) this (this)
    way (way)
Don't (don't) leave (leave) me (me) this (this)
    way (way)

Searching here and there...
Yet getting nowhere...
Don't leave me this way
For I know that you will carry me through
Your face will shine through the morning dew...
No matter what may come
I need you in front of me...

Dear Lord,
Help me not to go astray
Help me to find my way
Out of darkness Lord
For I will never doubt in your
Word. Oh Lord I wanna be heard, Oh...

Don't leave me this way
Oh Lord, don't leave me this way
I need you every minute of the day

Don't leave me this way
Stricken with sin
I know I can't win
I can't do it all by myself
Don't leave me this way

Please Lord, I need you in my life
In you I will abide
Thank You, Jesus

I will not leave you comfortless; I will come to you.
St. John 14:18

I will never leave thee,
nor forsake thee
Hebrews 13:5

WILL BE FREE

Will be free...
Will be free...
Will be free..., Someday

Someday out there will be free
If only we can see God's way,
There is gonna be a great falling
    on the way

Will be free of heartaches
Will be free of backaches

Suffer no pain
Through shine and rain
Will be able to find peace of mind

Will be free from Hell
There will not be anytime for wailing

God set me free from myself
For I know he will deliver me
If I ask him to, Lord with all
    sincerity

Will be free from every care
Will be free to share (God's Love)
For ever more (it's yours)

I need you to complete my life
    from guilt
I need you to confirm my soul...
    to understand thy light

Lord, I want to be free
    from desolation (destruction)
Lord, I want to be able
    to fill your compassion for my
    soul (You made me whole)
(more)

Will be free from all sorrows
Will be free of the morrow (following day)
He'll set you free out of the miry clay
I made a decision to live for...
You Lord, and I'll spread you word
in every way that I can (that I can)
Give me hope to be free again

I will be free again
Ah, ah, ah, ah again
You want to be free again
Trust and obey
His commandments
You will receive the Holy spirit
You will be free from worries that
oppressed you

Will be free...
You will be free...
Will be free...
I will be free again

Ad-lib

If the son therefore shall make you free, ye shall
be free indeed
John 8:36

Restore unto me the joy of thy salvation; and uphold
me with thy free spirit
Psalms 51:12

SATISFIED WITH YOURSELF

VERSE I:
A false balance is abomination to the Lord
But just weight is his delight

VERSE II:
When pride come... Then come... shame...
But with the lowly is wisdom

VERSE III
The integrity of the upright shall guide them
But the perseverance of transgressors shall destroy them

SOLOIST

If you ask God to direct your wicked ways to the
path of righteousness
(The Lord above) Oh, yes (He'll give you love)
(yes He will) Oh, yes (I know He will)
He will make your life content in Him
(Your life content in Him)

BACKGROUND
(Are you satisfied with yourself?)
(Are you satisfied with yourself?)
If you are satisfied with yourself
You can do for others as others do for you
(Oh, oh, oh yes)

VERSE IV
The righteousness of the upright shall
    deliver them
But transgressors shall be taken in their
    own naughtiness

VERSE V
There is that scattered... and yet increased...
    and there is that withheld more than is meet
But it tendeth to poverty
(more)

BACKGROUND
(Are you satisfied with yourself?)
(Are you satisfied with yourself?)

SOLOIST
Glorify the lord of my soul
For He has been so good to you
Jesus Christ our Savior died on calvary
For you and me that we may not live in
    iniquities

Are you satisfied, are you satisfied
    with yourself?
If you are...
Why don't you give God the praise?
May your heart not be dismayed
So be contented with Jesus
He will make a way

Are you satisfied of what you hear
    and see?
For the Lord is good to you and me

Taste Him and you will live in Him
Forevermore (forevermore...)
There will be no more sorrows (sorrows)

BRIDGE
Oh, are you satisfied (today)
With yourself? (with yourself)
Oh, so satisfied with myself (today)
Oh, so satisfied
Oh, satisfied, Oh I can see...
Oh, satisfied, Oh my heart is pleased...
Oh, satisfied, Oh my soul is in need...
Of shield security (shield security)
I need you Jesus (to feel complete)
I won't be satisfied
I am going to stay in this race
Until I can see His face
In you Lord, I have a higher, higher pace
To go on I am yours forevermore
For I will have no more sorrows
To call my own
In God I will press on

Oh I am satisfied
Oh so satisfied with myself now (Hallelujah)
Ad-lib (as you wish)

Lyricist Charles Jones
Inspired by Proverbs 11:2-6

JUST IN JESUS

Do you know Jesus Christ?
Did you know that He was the one?
The one who paid His price on
    Calvary for you and me.

Are you just in Jesus?
If you are honest and sincere
Give Him the glory
For it is such a right thing to do
No one can disapprove your love for Jesus
For he is such a Great King to all that is just.

Are you just in Christ?
For He died to save our lives
(Yes, he did!) For I know that
I will heed to everyone of His commands.
Whenever He demands (I will justify)

(Just) yourself in (Jesus)
(Just) yourself in (Jesus) Oh for...
It will be the best thing to do
It will bring you joy
It will bring you happiness
Even bring you more blessings
Give God the praise to prove your love
And make it just in Jesus
For it is such a thing to do

Give your love to Jesus Christ
For He died for you and me
He paid his price on calvary
He bled and suffered so much
For it is such a thing to do
For yourself (give God the glory)
(Just) in (Jesus)
(Just) in (Jesus)
(more)

Child, be honest to yourself
Oh child, be upright in Jesus
It's the only way to be
All the day long
We do not have long
On this earth
It's not our home to call our own.

Oh, give God the praise
(I blessed you Lord)
Just yourself in Jesus
Just yourself in Jesus
It will get better
If we just stick together (Hallelujah)
Just in Jesus (Justify yourself in Christ)
For it is such a great thing to do.

For therein is righteousness of God revealed from faith
to faith: as it is written, the just shall live by faith
Romans 1: 17

HERE WALKING ALONE

Lyrics by Charles Jones

I am here walking this life alone.
I have no one to call my own.
I am here walking and moaning.
Hoping someone will come forth during
    the morning.

I need someone to, to understand my needs.
I need that someone who will understand
    my cipher of life.
I know I can go on fighting this old
    slither.
But, with the help of the Lord, we can
    overcome this old backslider.

I am waiting for you, Lord. For me to meet
    that special someone in my life.
To bear my sweet loving child...
God, I need you here.
To take away my fears.
("I need you Lord." "I can't continue
    all by myself." "I need your hand and
    loving care.")
So, I will wait on you, Lord
    in this lifetime.
Your first clicking hand will be my sign.
Your second hand of the hour will be my tower.
To make the first step. Surely I will make the next.

Bridge:

I am here waiting for you, Lord.
There is no place for me to go.
Hiding my fears and doubts
is tearing my whole heart apart.
For I need to win, whatever may come about...
I need you to impart my light.
(more)

So everything will seem clear to
  me...
I don't want to walk alone
It frails me.
It sometimes gets lonely.
So I'll wait on you, Lord.
I know I will employ my
  lonely needs,
If I heed every one of your
  commandments.
In which you commanded on the solid
  rock mountain...
Like a solid rock foundation...
Casting out uncleansed immoral behavior...
Lord, you are my inspiration...
Lord, you are my sweet compassion...
Lord, you are my consolation...
Lord, you are my satisfaction...
Lord, I don't want to stay here. If only
  to walk alone.

He is the Rock, his work is perfect: for all his ways judgement: a God of
Truth and without iniquity, just and right is he.
Deuteronomy 32: 4

THAT IS WHY I LOVE HIM

(Expressively) Honestly   Lyrics by Charles Jones

The Lord, Jesus is my soul
He turned me around and made me whole
(and cause of that)
That is why I Love Him...
My life is more manifested by the Lord, Jesus
He opens my heart and welcomed my soul and made me
Oh-so whole (yes, I'm a witness) yes, He did.
That is why I love Him...
My life is less dim and more complete
(and cause of that)
That is why I love Him...
The Lord, Jesus gave me peace within
He spoke these words to me, "Sin no more
I am all you need."
For that I will give Him the glory
he deserved
That is why I love Him...
I will be heard
You see,
I was
stricken with sin
I open my heart and soul
Confess with my mouth
He walked in (that is why I love him...)

Herein is love, not that we loved God, but
that he loved us, and sent his Son to be the
propitiation for our sins.
I John 4: 10

CONCENTRATE MY CHILD

Words by Charles Jones

There comes a time,
When you have to find your way
    (your way)
Your way out of sin
You can't win on your own
    (your own)
Concentrate my child
    (my child)
You need concentration my child
When there was destruction near
Concentrate my dear (my dear)
It may get rough (it may get rough)
It may get tough (it may get tough)
    Concentrate my child (my child)
(That's all you need and that will be
    enough)
If you love my Jesus everything will be
    alright
All you have to do is fight on until the
    end
In Jesus you can win (you can win)
And He will abide in you (abide in you)
I'll tell you why? Because I tried Him (Him)
Concentrate my child (my child)
It may get rough (get rough)
It may get tough (get tough)
That is all you need (all you need)
It will be enough (It will be enough)
If this question disturbs your mind
Kneel down and pray in time.
Do you know Jesus?
Do you? He will bring you through
Well, I am here to tell you
    that he can.

God said, "He would not put more on
you than you can bear. For
I am your yoke. It's my resting place.
Come lay your face."

(more)

37

Do you know Him?
Do you wanna know Him?
Concentrate my child
    (my child)
You will find your way
    (your way)

People here and there
Yet getting nowhere
Telling you different how to know God.

Concentrate (concentrate)
My child (my child)

It's up to you (up to you
To choose (to choose)
    to know Him
    (to know Him)
    for yourself
    (for yourself)
You cannot do it all by yourself
You have to seek the Kingdom of
God first and live forever more
    (forever more)
Concentrate my child
    (concentrate my child)
God will bless you my child
    (bless you) (my child)

If you are seeking in the Lord
Seek him with all your heart
Let the Holy Ghost power take control
Harken unto Jesus. Praise God
In the most high (He will abide)
Seek Him with eagerness
He will open doors to your
wretched heart
(He will cast out all wickedness)

Concentrate in the Lord
    make it yours
    weep it more
Concentrate, concentrate my child

(more)

Give Him all you got
You won't loose a lot
Concentrate (concentrate)
    my child (my child)
Concentrate (concentrate)
    my child (my child)
on Jesus
    (Jesus)

Concentrate on the Lord.
Concentrate on the spirit.
Concentrate on the power.
Concentrate on the Holy one.
Concentrate until He will make a way
Hallelujah, Hallelujah
I blessed ye, Lord
I need your love.
I need your power.
I need your spirit.
I need to pray.
I need to concentrate on you Lord.

Ad-lib

But seek ye first the kingdom of god, and his
righeousness; and all these things shall be added
unto you
St. Matthew 6:33

BE THANKFUL UNTO THEE

Inspired by Psalm 100

CHOIR:

Father, I thank thee
For each blessing to me every precious day

Father, I thank thee
For making a way for me to see each and everyday

Father, I thank thee
For my salvation and preparing my supplication

Father, I thank thee
For giving me preparation for
peace to live within you.

BACKGROUND:

Be thankful unto Thee
Be thankful unto Thee

SOLO:

For God so love the world, that
He gave his only begotten son to die
for our sins for you and me.
For that we should be thankful to Thee.
Let salvation come what may that
We should kneel down and pray
unto thee and be thankful
Through hardaches and pain
Even though sunshine and rain
Be thankful unto Thee unto God thy
Father.
Be thankful unto Thee
Be more complete than Thee.

SOLO: BRIDGE BACKGROUND:

For God is my witness
Be thankful unto Thee
Whom I serve with my spirit in the
gospel of His son.

Be thankful unto Thee
Without I ceasing I make mention
of you always in my prayers
Be thankful unto Thee

SOLO: BACKGROUND:

Be thankful unto Thee
For both to the wise and
to the unwise. Be thankful for Jesus
Be thankful unto Thee

SOLO:

For I am not ashamed of the gospel of Christ.
For it is the Power of God Unto
Salvation to every one who believeth in His word.
My Lord, you will be heard
by the Glory of God.
So be thankful unto Thee.

SOLO: BACKGROUND (second bridge):

Be thankful!
For what God has done
Be thankful!
For God gave his only son
Be thankful!
For what you got
Be thankful!
Even if you don't have a lot
Be thankful!
Through good times and bad times
Be thankful!
For God's miracles
Be thankful!
For Supernatural Power
Be thankful!
So be thankful for living to live
Be thankful!
Be thankful for giving to give

Ad-lib

THE TEN COMMANDMENTS

Transcribed by Charles Jones

I have a great story to tell everyone that livith on earth.

They shall never forget the Ten Commandments.

For God's law upon the earthly people should abide and have everlasting life.

God said, "Unto Moses go and speak unto the people."

God declared these words unto Moses.

"I am the Lord thy God, which have brought thee out of the land of Egypt, out of the house of bondage.

Thou shalt have no other gods before me

Thou shalt not make unto thee any graven image, or any likeness of any thing that is in heaven above.

For I the Lord thy God am a jealous God.

Thou shalt not take the name of the Lord thy God in vain.

Remember the sabbath day, to keep it Holy. Six days shalt thou labor, and do all thy work.

Honor thy father and thy mother.

Thou shalt not kill.

Thou shalt not steal.

Thou shalt not bear false witness against thy neighbor.

When you hear or see the thundering and the lightning and the noise of the trumpet sound and the mountains smoking all around.

Fear not for God has come to prove to you and say sin not.

For this is the will of God...

Obey the Ten Commandments

(more)

Trust and obey God's will

For this is the will of God

We need to live a better life

For this will bring you out of darkness

And turn your nights into day.

For God will make a way

Just have faith

He'll give you pow'r

If you abide in him

Your days and nights will not seem dim.

Let us hear the conclusion of the whole matter: Fear God,
and keep his commandments: for this is the whole duty of man.
Try Him.
Ecclesiastes 12:13

JUDGMENT DAY

Vital (with all heart)   Words by Charles Jones

For to this end Christ both died, and
    rose and revived, that he might be
    Lord both of the dead and living.
Why do we judge our brother?
For we shall stand before
    the judgment seat of Christ.

For it is written,
As I live,
    saith the Lord.
Every knee shall bow to me
    and every tongue shall confess to God.

So than everyone (I mean everyone)
    of us shall give account of himself
    to God.

Let us not therefore judge one
    another any more.
But judge this rather,
that no man put a stumbling block
or an occasion to fall in his brother's way.

We don't have time to waste
    our life away (life away)
So you better get ready for Jesus
He'll make a way
    (make a way) a way (for you)
    yes he will
    (yes he will)
Slow not your heart, Trust and Obey
    trust and obey)
In the Lord. We don't have time
His time is not our time on earth
I know that for a fact today
Believe within your heart that Christ is
the way (Christ is the way...)

                           (more)

CHORUS

Giving Him what you got
And forward your lot
Your soul will be saved
Christ will never forsake
                    Because...
Judgment Day is almost nigh
        Do not ask me why
No one knows the day nor the hour
        of Christ return
Only Judgment Day knows
        Get ready before it's to late

(fade quietly)

(Judgment Day is coming soon...)
(Judgment Day is coming soon...)
(Judgment Day is coming soon...)
(Judgment Day is coming soon...)

I am Alpha and Omega, the beginning
and the ending, saith the Lord, which is,
was, and which is to come, the Almighty.
Revelation 1: 8

PSALM 35

Transcribed by Charles Jones

Plead my cause. O Lord,
with them that strive with me
(fight against them that fight against me).
Take hold of shield and buckler,
And stand up for mine help.
(Stop the way against them that
persecute me) say unto my soul.
I am thy salvation.
And my soul shall be joyful in
the Lord (it shall rejoice in his
salvation).

Oh, oh, oh Lord deliver me
from destruction.
Deliver me, deliver me (me)
from supplication.
Deliver me, yes, deliver me
from pain and sorrows.
Deliver me, yes, please deliver me
from sickness and iniquities.
Oh, oh, oh Lord deliver me
far above all wickedness.

Let us shout for joy.
Let us shout for happiness.
And be glad, that favor my righteous
cause.
Let the Lord be magnified.
And my tongue shall speak of
Thy righteousness and of Thy
praise all the day long.

PSALM 117, 118

Transcribed by Charles Jones

O give thanks unto the Lord;
For He is good, cause His mercy
endureth forever.

O give thanks unto the Lord;
For he is good.
Give thanks from your heart to the Lord,
cause his mercy endures forever.

Give thanks to God.
Give thanks from your heart.
Give God every part of you
Shall it be the glory to the Lord.

O praise the Lord
    all ye nations.
Praise Him,
    all ye people.
For His merciful kindness is great toward
us and the truth of the Lord endureth forever.

O give thanks unto the Lord;
For He is good.
For His mercy endureth forever.
Praise ye the Lord.

HE IS COMING SOON

He is coming soon.
He is coming soon.
He is coming soon...

There is no maybe.
There is no might.

He is coming soon.
He is coming soon.
He is coming soon...

He is coming soon to do God's will.
He is coming soon.
As he said, in His Word
And the world will know who is the righteous.

He is coming soon.
He is coming soon.

No one knows the day nor the hour.
Of Christ's return from Heaven.
Only judgment day know what's right.
For He is on his way. For His people
Who made a way to see
and to stand on His Word.
He is coming back soon.
To all who are just in Him.
Your night will not seem so dim anymore.
For he is coming soon, very soon,
Oh soon.
He is coming soon. Oh, soon.
Rock's are going to cry out.
He is coming soon. Oh, soon.
He is coming soon.
Get ready before it's too late.
He is coming soon.
Give your heart and do not procrastinate.

He is coming soon.
He is coming soon.
He is coming soon.
He is coming soon.

Behold, I come quickly blessed is he that keepeth the sayings of the prophecy of this book
And behold, I come quickly; and my reward is with me to give every man according as his work shall be He which testifieth these things saith, surely I come quickly Amen. Even so, come. Lord Jesus
Revelation 22: 7,12,20

48

GONNA MEND MY WAYS

Lyrics by Charles Jones

Here I go again
Here thinking I can do the things
Whether it's right or wrong.

But how can I go on
Like this much longer and suffer

I need a new heart.
I need a new mind.
I need a new body.

Pretending to be what others
see that I am not...

This life remains confusing at times
But I believe it's in the mind of what
we want to see and be.

Lord above can change our
ways to be profound and
I believe one day the Son of the Father
will soon come down and mend our ways
if we fast and pray.
If we
Stick together
Like feathers of a bird
And fly high beyond the sky

Gonna mend my ways
Gonna mend my ways
Gonna mend my ways (with the help of Jesus)

Pretending to be what I am
not killing my mind
Tearing my sensitive heart apart.

(more)

49

<u>CHORUS</u>: repeat

Gonna mend my ways
Gonna mend my ways
Gonna mend my ways
    (with the help of Jesus Christ)

If anyone can understand
how I feel
Please... make that stand
And... take my hand.

In all this mess
that came about my way
will someday pass away.

Sometimes I speak to my
God and I ask
"Why this happen to me
I watch, fight and pray
without ceasing all day...

Until my God says rest
upon his breast

I want to live and be free
from wicked ways again
again...

To experience a new beginning
starting all over from the start
and this time do it right.

Gonna mend my ways
From the wrong way
Gonna walk a straight and
Righteous path and
Never fall because...
I' m gonna mend my ways .
I said to myself "what is the right
way. Is it to love someone with
the love of the Lord."

Everything will fall in place
If I stay in the race.

and he will teach us of his ways,
and we will walk in his path:
Isaiah 2:3

50

I, TOO, LOVE YOU

Lyrics by Charles Jones
Inspired by St. Matthew 23:37

I, too
Can love you with all my heart
I, too
Can love you and never will depart
I, too
Feel my soul for you
I, too
Can be like you
I, too
Need you in my life
I, too
Need your loving spirit
I, too
Care for you
I, too
Know you will make a way
I, too
Desire for your Holy Word
I, too
Live to live again in you
I, too
Give to give again in you
I, too
Long for my heavenly home
I, too
Trust and obey your word
I, too
Love you with my heart
I, too
Will put all my trust in you.

I, too, Love you
I, too, Love you
I, too, Love you   Lord...

I, too, can love you
I, too, can love you
I, too, can love youJesus...

I, too
Know you will arrive on time and
make everything all right.

51

DREAMING ALL DAY LONG

Lyrics by Charles Jones

What if the world had peace?
What would we do with it?

What if the world suddenly
start caring for one another as we are?
What a blessing it would be.

What if the world give to one another
in time? If they need.
What a blessing it would be.

What if the world
love one another no matter
What we are?
Just as Jesus.

What if the world stop
fighting one in another in time?

What if the world would
start seeing God's way?
For it's good news.

Would this be all grand?
Is this a dream we dreamt
all the day long?

Dreaming all the day long about a
world God created in the
beginning and end.

Will someday ever we put down
our weapons and see God's way
and not in our own understanding?

He'll surely make your day comfort
and whole.

(more)

In bad dreams
In good dreams
Right and wrong dreams
He'll surely beam a bright
light upon the mind...

Dreaming all the day long
Is surely not wrong
Dreaming all the day long
For peaceful sweet song.

Dreaming all the day long
Dreaming all the day long
For something peaceful and enduring
forever as we hope for

Dreaming, dreaming for a special
place
Dreaming, dreaming for a special
time to see His face.

Dreaming, Dreaming
All the day long
Dreaming, dreaming
All the day long.

And it shall come to pass afterward, that I will
Pour out my spirit upon all flesh; and yours
sons daughters shall prophesy ,your old men
shall dream dreams, your young men shall see
visions
Joel 2:2

WHERE WOULD I BE?

Lyrics by Charles Jones

Where would I be
If it had not been for Jesus Christ
Where would I be
If it had not been for Him
Where would I be
Where would I be (tell me where)
I was lost so deep in sin
When He took me in
My life was all wrapped up in sin
Where would I be
If God had not made me realize
my past life   Now...
It was all left up to me
To be where I want to be.

He made me know who was righteous
For my sake
He show me day from night
For my sake
He saved me and called upon me to hear
The word of a new beginning
For my sake
He gave me strength from being weary
So, where would I be
If the devil had made me swallow
his power.

But I,
Thank God, for saving my soul from falling
In a trap I could not solve on my own.

Where would I be
Where would I be
Where would I be
If had not been for Him.

Where would I be
Where would I be
Where would I be
If it had not been for Jesus Christ.

IN PRAYER

Lyrics by Charles Jones

When everything around me goes
wrong;
I know the Lord will make me
strong in prayer...

When sometimes my days and nights
seems awfully dim;
I know I can go to Him
in prayer...

When tears fall upon my face,
He's letting me know I can take
the pain and stay in the race
in prayer...

In the midnight hours I can
go to my God in prayer.

Bridge:

Patiently I wait
on the Lord   Cause...
I know he will
never fail
My prayer is in His heart
His love to me will never depart.

Nothing like a sweet word of prayer
reaching high
Nothing like a sweet word of prayer
soaring high.

To my sweet-smelling Jesus
From Him all blessings flow
In the river where heart's floods
So, remember to say your prayer
Fast not with a wretched heart.
Give all hope and glory and never
doubt in His word.

And it come to pass in those
days, that he went out into a
moutain to pray , and
continued all night in
prayer to God
St. Luke 6:12

55

LET'S SING PRAISES

Lyrics by Charles Jones

Let's sing praises
Let's sing praises
For he is worthy to be praised
Let's sing praises
To the Lord, Our Lord Jesus Christ

Let's sing praises
Let's sing praises
To the Lord
For He is worthy to be praised.

Let's sing
Let's sing
Let's sing   praises...

Let's sing praises
Let's sing praises
Everybody sing   Hallelujah!
                   Hallelujah!
                   Hallelujah!

Make a joyful noise unto the Lord, all the earth: make a loud
Noise, and rejoice, and sing praise.
Psalms 149: 3

PRAISE, PRAISE

(Psalm 150)

Transcribed by Charles Jones

Praise ye the Lord.
Praise God in His Sanctuary,
Praise Him in the firmament of His power.
Praise Him for His mighty acts;
Praise Him according to His excellent greatness.
Praise Him with the sound of the trumpet,
Praise Him with the psalmery and harp.
Praise Him with the timbrel and dance,
Praise Him with stringed instruments and organs.
Praise Him upon the loud cymbals,
Praise Him upon the high sounding cymbals.
Let every thing that hath breath
praise the Lord, praise ye the Lord.

Chorus:

Praise, praise, praise,
Let His name reign.
Praise, praise, praise
Let Him name reign.
Praise ye the Lord...

PSALM 33

Transcribed by Charles Jones

Rejoice in the Lord, O you righteous
Praise befits the upright.
Praise the Lord with the lyre,
Make melody to Him with the harp of ten strings.
Sing to him a new song.
Play skillfully on the strings, with loud shouts.

For the Word of the Lord is upright,
and all his work is done in faithfulness.
He loves righteousness and justice;
the earth is full of the steadfast love of the Lord.

Let all the earth fear the Lord
Let all the inhabitants of the
    world stand in awe of him...
For He spoke, and it came to be
    He commanded, and it stood forth.

Our soul waits for the Lord
He is our help and shield
Yea, our heart is glad in Him
because we trust in His Holy name
Let Thy steadfast love, O Lord, be upon us
even as we hope in Thee...

PSALM 49

Transcribed by Charles Jones

Hear this, all peoples
Give ear, all inhabitants of the world,
both low and high
rich and poor together.
My mouth shall speak wisdom;
The mediation of my heart shall be understanding.
I will incline my ear to a proverb
I will solve my riddle to the music of the lyre.

PSALM 51

Transcribed by Charles Jones

Have mercy on me, O God
according to Thy steadfast love
Wash me thoroughly from my iniquity,
and cleanse me rom my sin.

For I know my transgressions,
and my sin is ever before me.

Behold, I was brought forth in iniquity
and in sin did my mother conceive me.
Behold, though desired truth in the inward being;
therefore teach me wisdom in my secret heart.
Purge me with hyssop, and I shall be clean;
wash me, and I shall be whiter than snow.
Fill me with joy and gladness.

Create in me a clean heart, O God,
and put a new and right spirit within me.
Cast me not away from Thy presence
and take not Thy Holy Spirit from me
Restore to me the Joy of Thy salvation
and uphold me with a willing spirit.

Then I will teach transgressors Thy
ways, and sinners will return to Thee.
Deliver me from blood guiltiness, O God,
Thou God of my salvation,
and my tongue sing aloud of Thy deliverance.

PRAISE THE LORD

(Psalm 117)

Transcribed by Charles Jones

O praise the Lord, all ye nations
praise him, all ye people
For His merciful, kindness is great toward
us: and the truth of the Lord endureth
forever.

Praise ye the Lord, nation
Praise ye the Lord, people
Praise ye the Lord, land
Praise ye the lord,
With your heart... with your heart.

HOW EXCELLENT IS THY NAME

Lyrics by Charles Jones

O Lord Our Lord, How excellent is thy name
    in all the earth
O Lord Our Lord, How excellent is thy name
    in all the earth

His name shall reign forevermore
    in glory
His name shall reign forevermore
    in glory.

How excellent is thy name
It's more precious than pure gold
How excellent is thy name
It's more precious than pure gold.

How excellent is thy lovingkindness, O
God! Therefore the children of men put
their trust under the shadow of thy wings
Psalms 36:7

HOLY, HOLY

Lyrics by Charles Jones

Holy, Holy, Holy
   Holy, Holy, Holy
      Yes, He is Holy.

He is the Righteous One
He is the Holy one.

Holy, Holy, Holy
   Holy, Holy, Holy
      Yes, He is Holy.

He is a righteous one
He is the Holy one

I shall live my Life Holy
I shall live forever more Holy
in Jesus Christ
For He is Holy and Righteous

I worship toward thy holy temple
Psalm 5:7

63

LIFT HIM HIGH

Lyrics by Charles Jones

Life Him high
Lift Him high
   Oh so high!

Lift my Savior high
Lift Him high.

Lift Him high
Lift Him high
Lift my Savior high
Lift Him high
   Oh so high!

Oh lift Him up
Oh lift Him up.

Glory be Thy name
Glory be Thy name
   Oh lift Him high
   Oh lift Him high!

O GIVE THANKS (UNTO THE LORD)

Lyrics by Charles Jones

O give thanks upon the Lord for He is good;
For His mercy endureth forever.

O give thanks unto the God of gods;
For His mercy endureth forever.

O give thanks to the Lord of lords;
For his mercy endureth forever.

O give thanks
O give thanks
O give thanks
Unto the Lord.

TIME WILL TELL

Lyrics by Charles Jones

Someday Jesus Christ
    shall return from Heaven,
To inform His true story.

Someday Jesus Christ
    shall return from Heaven,
To inform His true story.

Time will tell
    when Jesus Christ return
    from Heaven.
Time will tell
    when Jesus Christ return
    from Heaven.

No one knows the day
nor the hour when Christ return.

Only time will tell
when Christ returns.

GIVE THANKS

Lyrics by Charles Jones

I will give thanks to the Lord with my whole heart.
I will tell of all Thy wonderful deeds.
I will sing praises to Thy name, O Most High.

Sing praises to God, sing praises: sing praises
Unto our King, sing praises.
Psalms 47: 6

HE IS THE ONE

Lyrics by Charles Jones

God will be there
Whenever you need Him

Oh He is the one
Who will set your heart free
He is the one
Who died on the hill of Calvary
He is the one
Who gives peace and harmony
He is the one
Oh-He is the one He is...
The Holy One.

He is the one
He is the one

Let's give God the praises
He is the one
He is worthy to be praised
He is the one
The Holy One
He is the one.

He is the one (Holy One)
He is the Holy one
God is the one

I'LL TRY AGAIN

Lyrics by Charles Jones

Looking up to the Lord
I say to myself is there anyway
for me to make it after all
when I fall. I call on your name
to fast and pray
     and try again...

When fear forth my path
knowledge above gives me a song
to sing with grace so divine
I must try again.

I'll try again when I fall
I'll try again give me all
I must try again
when my Jesus call
I know I can make it after all.

Surely goodness, I must try again
to make it after all.

That ye might walk worthy of the Lord
unto all pleasing being fruitful in every
good work, and increasing in knowledge
of God; strengthened with all might,
 according to his glorious power, unto all
patience and longsuffering with joyfulness.
Colossians 1: 10-11

DON'T HOLD BACK

Lyrics by Charles Jones

Don't stop right there!
Don't give up on yourself, my child
(Heaven standing at your side)

...I remember mama sayin,
"My child whatever gonna
become of you. If you
hold back..."

Give yourself to Jesus
He'll make it easy
Don't hold back your feelings
Believing in yourself
being all that you can be and
nothing else can fake it's way
to the top (He provides the lot)
Whatever your plot.
Don't hold back
Mountain you must climb
Don't hold back
Mountain you must climb
Don't hold back
Bridge over trouble water you must cross

Don't hold back
Your life to the course of destruction
Don't hold back down
Below there's fire
God is your desire

He sacrificed
Gave his all
That we might
Give our all
One day set us free
Able to the majesty

FEEL MY LOVE

Lyrics by Charles Jones

Lord, God Almighty
Hear my word through the
love of my heart

You and only you possesses my soul
When I feel discouraged and gray.
My heart means to obey
in your word

I stand before your present
Still on my knees
For you and only you to
Feel my love
Feel my love, in need of your love

Moments come
Moments go
I extend my love I have for you
Giving tender moments of your
precious love grows in me.
Feel my love
Feel my love
Standing here
Standing now
Feel my love
From below
goes to you (only you)

(soft spoken)

Feel my love...

A PRAYER TO GOD

Dear Lord, I feel deprived in my soul. Please help me to overcome the agonizing pain that I have suffered in life.

To those who do not care, show them the light and make their fellowship bright through your amplified power among all creeds, the afflicted, and all nationalities.

I pray on and on in your name, Lord, asking forgiveness by confession, that my soul may be purified and my vision may be focused on the light of your spirit. Lord, also, freshen my tongue so that I may speak your name wisely. Speak to me, Lord, in my ear so that I may perceive sounds and heed every command of your precious voice.

All this I ask in the name of they son, Jesus. Amen.

Charles Jones

Believest thou not that I am in the Father,
And the Father in me? The words that I speak
Not of myself: but the Father that dwelleth in me,
he doeth the works.
John 14 : 10

Chapter 2
SCRIPTURES FROM THE
HOLY BIBLE_{kjv}

Researcher,

Charles Jones

SCRIPTURES FROM THE HOLY BIBLE

THE LOVE OF CHRIST

Romans 8:35

"Who shall separate us from the love of Christ."

IT IS THE GIFT OF GOD

Ephesians 2:8,9

"For by grace are ye saved through faith; and that not of yourselves. It is the gift of God. Not of works, least any man should boast."

Romans 10:17

"Faith cometh by hearing, and hearing by the word of God."

Ephesians 6:24

"Grace be with all them that love our Lord Jesus Christ in sincerity. Amen."

WANT A WORSHIPFUL MOOD

Psalm 84

"O Lord God of hosts, hear my prayer; give ear."

Psalm 116

"I love the Lord, because he hath heard my voice and my supplications. Because he hath inclined his ear unto me. Therefore will I call upon him as long as I live."

St. John 4:24

"God is a Spirit: and they that worship him must worship him in spirit and in truth."

(move)

YOU ARE WEARY

St. Matthew 11:28,30

"Come unto me, all ye that labor and are heavy laden, and I will give you rest. For my yoke is easy and my burden is light."

DESTITUTE

Proverbs 15:21,24,33

"Folly is joy to him is destitute of wisdom; but a man of understanding walketh uprightly."

"The way of life is above to the wise, that he may depart from hell beneath."

"The fear of the Lord is the instruction of wisdom; and before honor is humility."

St. John 3:16

"For God so loved the world, that he gave his only begotten Son. That whosoever believeth in him should not perish, but have everlasting life."

Psalm 23:6

"Surely goodness and mercy shall follow me all the days of my life, and I will dwell in the house of the Lord forever. Amen."

Those who learn, learn more.

Charles Jones

BEAR A GRUDGE

"Love one another as we are." We're all the same, but different in many ways.

Charles Jones

"Therefore seeing we have this ministry, as we have received mercy, we faint not, but have renounced the hidden things of dishonestly, not walking in craftiness, nor handling the word of God deceitfully; but, by manifestation of the truth, commending ourselves to every man's consequence in the sight of God.

"But if our gospel be hid, it is hid to them that are lost. In whom the God of this world hath blended the minds of them which believe not, lest the light of the glorious gospel of Christ, who is the image of God, should shine unto them.

"For we preach not ourselves, but Christ, Jesus the Lord; and ourselves your servants for Jesus' sake."

II Corinthians 4:2,3,4,5

NEW THOUGHTS

and if there be any praise, think on these things

Philippians 4:8

Give yourself time to think, what's next?
The mind really deserves time to think
ad what we need is new thought.
Some say, *"It's impossible to think positively*
when there's so much turmoil and famine on earth
surrounding our hearts and minds."
A new thought can take you far off into a peculiar place.
Once your new thoughts develop,
the words you say will become much clearer in your mind.
The mind is a terrible thing to waste.
When your mind is involved in negative settings,
how can you cooperative with society?
It will become impossible to maintain relationships with others.
For instance, you cannot go around being mad or angry with your brothers and sisters.
You know that holding a grudge against someone can lead to internal pain and rage.
In the Bible God said to love one another as He loves us.
I tell you negative thoughts will drain an individual, mentally and physically.
Plan your days to put God first in your life
and focus your thoughts and abilities through Him.
When you think beyond the bigger picture, you're thinking outside the box.
Remember, there is a secret place you can go to pray with the Son unto the Father.
We all should have an investment in property where we can pray alone.
God is love and holy. He identifies us as his own because He paid a price
so we would have a release on debt.
Give yourself time to know him.
He is a real friend you can truly depend on.
Trust your new thoughts on Him to cultivate in your life.
God wonderfully made us in His image, to rise above any circumstances
When they come rolling in one by one.
He is daily good news to read and follow. Feed on Him.
Your mind can use some stimulation to operate your heart, body, and soul.
Keep those thoughts pure
and together you will bond forever
under the Will of God.

Chapter 3
WORDS
OF
PLEASURE

By Charles Jones

SAVING GRACE

Saving Grace, how sweet the sound. One day, I will be receiving.

I was once lost. Thank God, I am found was blind and now I see.

It was that saving grace, God has for me.

And I will one day hear him say,

"Well done, well done my child, my child."

Now I know he loves me.

Thank You, Jesus, for saving my soul.

The grace of our Lord Jesus Christ
be with you all Amen
Revelation 22:21

GRACE

(Grace of our Lord)

"For ye know the grace of our Lord Jesus Christ, that, though he was rich, yet for your sakes he became poor, that ye through his poverty might be rich."

II Corinthians 8:9

(Singing with grace in heart)

"And above all these things put on charity, which is the bond of perfectness.
"And let the peace of God rule in your hearts, to the which also ye are called in one body; and be ye thankful.
"Let the word of Christ dwell in you richly in all wisdom; teaching and admonishing one another in psalms and hymns and spiritual songs, singing with grace in your hearts to the Lord.
"And whatsoever ye do in word or deed, do all in the name of the Lord Jesus, giving thanks of God and the Father by him."

Colossians 3:14-17

"Likewise, ye younger, submit yourselves unto the elder. Yea, all of you be subject one to another, and be clothed with humility; for God resisteth the proud, and giveth grace to the humble."

I Peter 5:5

"The salutation by the hand of me Paul. Remember my bonds. Grace be with you. Amen."

Colossians 4:18

Researcher,

Charles Jones

❧DIFFERENT GOALS IN LIFE❧

Some people's goals are different in many ways. Just to name a few....

Some people are striving to make it to heaven as they say honest from their heart.

Well...

Some people striving to be the very best in life with God's Help. (That's good.)

Some people striving in their jobs and career heights. I guess that's normal.

(What is normal?) Oxford defines it correctly in its own way (2. free from mental or emotional disorders)

I say I believe normal is God of salvation.

Something to think about may possibly be true. It's your belief...

I believe the Lord Jesus' goal is to save his people when he returns from heaven.

(What is heaven?) Oxford defines it correctly in its own way (3. a place or state of supreme bliss, something delightful)

"I believe heaven is the building of God, a house not made with hands, eternal in heavens."

Corinthians 5:1

God, the Father's goal is to say "Well done, my child, to each and everyone of us personally."

Let's give God the praise and manifest in Him all right. May God bless you in every way.

Goals in Life
Writing by ✍
Charles Jones

"WELL DONE"

"Well done." That's what He'll say.
Well done, my child. For you have obeyed
unto my words. When you gave your all.
I gave my saving grace unto you.

✍ Writer, "Well Done"
Charles A. Jones

His lord said unto him, Well done, good and faithful servant;
Thou hast been faithful over a few things, I will make thee ruler
over many things: enter thou into the joy of thy lord
St. Matthew 25: 21 kjv

Chapter 4
⅀ TRADITIONAL STORY OF A CHURCH SERVICE
CHURCH ⅀
ONE SUNDAY MORNING

ONE SUNDAY MORNING

One Sunday morning, on September 27, 1977, I gathered my Sunday church clothes, my very best clothes, and went to church. During the Sunday school lesson I learned that the love of Christ is the finest in all of the world.

Marching on...after Sunday school, I attended the eleven o'clock service. I heard the preacher say, "Love thy brethren (I John 3:14). He serviced the subject of love thy brother saith the Lord God. He opened the Bible and quoted a scripture (I John 4:21) that reflected my life. What a difference that Sunday made inside of me! I felt the Holy Spirit, which anointed me. He conquered my love toward all men that are both for and against me.

Then came the Mount Holy choir. They were like angels from Heaven, singing all praises to the Lord Jesus. The selection the choir sang titled "God's Angels are Here All the Time," comforted my soul and made my heart humble with love and serenity.

We sing and shout the glory to God the Father. We sing praises to Alpha and Omega, Messiah Jehovah, Jireh, thanks to the Lord Jesus for saving my soul from hell, eternal hell.

Hallelujah, hallelujah, hallelujah, praise him, praise him, alleluia, alleluia, alleluia, praise him, praise him, the beginning and the end.

Time is moving onto devotion. The Deacon gathers two men from the board of trustees to sing and pray, to pray all men unto God, to wash their sinful ways white as snow,

Who all wants to go to that great land where there is no sorrow, no homelessness or hungry people in need, no rich nor poor people on the promised land,

Nothing but pure dedicated souls devoted to God in prayer.

Give yourself in prayer, give a kind offering and tithes, may the kind offering be a blessing to the church youth and adult choir and we will be blessed with the communion (in remembrance of Jesus Christ Our Savior) this Sunday night at 7:30 pm.

May the church rise in prayer, Dear Lord, the church needs to survive and stay alive.

This evening the Christians and saints are gathering, an offering and tithes in love and kindness from their heart. This church is filled with the Holy Spirit every Sunday morning, noon and night.

The prayer continues: In glory to the King of kings, God of gods, Lord of lords, have mercy upon my weary soul.

Thank you for your kind offerings, you may be seated.

Time for Sister Rosa Johnson, Secretary of the Treasury, to announce the Sunday message bulletin for this week and the coming Sunday, the second Sunday.

May the church rise for closing in prayer. May God bless you and your family. We thank you for coming to our service. We hope in Jesus Christ you had a wonderful time. Remember God our Lord loves and adores you. He cares and knows our burdens we carry all the day long.

God bless and good night. Amen. ✝

"One thing I've learned about going to church.
God has sustained exceedingly and abundantly
Spiritual wealth in my soul, for its not a day
being a Christian, I don't experience the Holy Spirit
Conviction."

Charles

And Jesus, walking by the sea of Galilee, saw two brethren, Simon
Called Peter, and Andrew his brother, casting a net into the sea: for they
Were fishers. And he saith unto them, Follow me, and I will make you fishers of men.
Matthew 4: 18-19

Not forsaking the assembling of ourselves
together, as the manner of some is; but
exhorting one another: and so much the
move, as ye see the day approaching
Hebrews 10:25

So that we ourselves glory in you in the churches of God for your patience
And faith in all your persecutions and tribulation that ye endure
Thessalonians 1:4

I BELIEVE (IN A MAN CALLED JESUS)

I believe in a man name Jesus
He's the Son of God, Almighty One
I believe in a man name Jesus
His words have truly blessed and strengthen me
He is the living water I drink everyday
He is the bread that feeds my hungry soul in need
I believe I can stand on his name
And never lose my mind and soul.

I believe when I'm down and weary
He carries the load my heart's heavy burden
I truly believe he's there and cares about me.

CHORUS:
I believe in a man name Jesus
He is the Son of God, Almighty One
I believe in a man name Jesus
I believe in a man name Jesus
I believe, I truly believe, believe,
believe, I believe.
Do you believe? I believe.
Do you wanna believe in the man name Jesus?
Who will never fail, no, not him, no, not him.

I trust and I believe He heals the sick in need
I believe truly, I believe everyday of my life
He's there, right there to calm your fears,
when tears overflow in your eyes, he's always near.

Friends and loved ones say, "Who do you believe?"
I say to them, "Jesus, the Son of God Almighty spirit
Lord with authority."
One say, "Why?" I tell them,
He cast all sin out of me when I pray with all sincere
I ask the Lord Jesus to see and care for my needs
I believe in his words and stand on solid rock
Standing on the solid rock I can see from afar
as I believe Jesus will return from heaven...
(more)

That is why I believe in the Lord Jesus,
God almighty, Lord with the authority
I believe and I stand in the promise of
Your word that never dies.

People live and die believing and not believing
In the One, the Holy One, no way can they
call on His name without believing in the word
and survive the sinful world
We all need to believe
We can stand, believing eternity.

I believe that Jesus Christ is the son of God
Acts 8:37

And this is his commandment, That we should believe on the
Name of his Son Jesus Christ, and love one another, as he gave
us commandment.
I John 3: 23

FRIEND OF GOD

Words by Charles Jones

Solemnly believed...

Now listen, please! Listen. You can be a friend of God.

Now listen, please! Listen. Declare yourself to Jesus for supplication of salvation.

To the righteous, for he cares and knows everything we're going through in this moment of time.

You really need someone who surely will come when you're down and low.

And this friend whose side was riven and inboard. (Whose side was riven) (and inboard)

We need to relate ourselves more honestly unto God for He is all things in creativity.

Beginning and end. (beginning and end)

A real friend made unto God. His name was Abraham who was descendant a son called Isaac.

His name was Abraham who was descendent a son called Isaac...
To explicate:

(In the scripture of James 2:23 verse its speaks of faith without work called the friend of God...)

And the Scripture was fulfilled which said, Abraham believed God, and it was imputed unto him for righteousness and he was called the friend of God.

A truth of Abraham was called God. God promised Abraham a son. Because he believed with faith and not works alone.

His faith was strong and alive, living well. Thank God. (Thank God) for this example that we should believe for all things are possible according to God.

Remember God is a real friend. For as the body without the spirit is dead. And so faith without works is dead also.

(more)

You can too, be a friend of God. Sure your trust in Him.
Give your heart. May it be filled with love and joy

You can too be a friend of the creator of Kings of kings.
Trust and obey the Lord for all things are possible to happen in a life time.

My God, the Father. He is so kind and wonderful.
I blessed you, Lord.

Chapter 5

KEEP
A
JOURNAL
IN YOUR
DAILY
WALK...

Journal

❧ Discover Poetry Inside Of You ❧

Chapter 6
BALANCED YOUR LIFE

Just weight person
Is a balanced person
Who walks in the light
Of the Lord, Jesus Christ
Our Savior. Amen.

The way of the just is uprightness: thou, most
Upright, dost weigh the path of the just.
Isaiah 26:7

SPIRIT

Don't let any man
nor wicked spirit
deprive you of your
Precious Holy Spirit
that God lies in you.
In the Name of Jesus Christ,
Our Savior, Lord Amen.

Now we have received, not the
spirit of the world, but the spirit
which of God; that we might
know the things are freely given
to us of God
I Corinthians 2:12

HOLY SPIRIT

Will you toss your troubles aside?
And take a minute or two
to feel the Holy Spirit in you?
Feeling the Sensational Spirit
is very needy to the soul
to feel full and complete
In this society we live in today
the Spirit will make a way
Marvelous the Spirit lives
Electrifying the Spirit wonders
Pleasure the Spirit gives to my soul.

Spirit of love
is pleasing to the heart of mankind
Spirit of truth
is honesty during the test of times
Spirit of faith
is trusting in God and His love is mine
Spirit of peace
is freedom to unite nations under the
Kingdom of God.

Amen.

What? Know ye not that your
body is the temple of the Holy Ghost
which is in you, which ye have of
God, and ye are not your own ?
For ye are bought with a price:
therefore glorify God in your body,
and in your spirit, which are God's
I Corinthians 6: 19-20

DEAR GOD, OUR FATHER

There comes a time in our lives when we must take a real good look at reality;
A real good look at ourselves in the mirror, as we are.

There is something beautiful within us, There is music playing and singing within us all the time.
We must allow it to play loudly and softly in us.

We have sweet love hangovers when we read God's word, His holy word, We have peace like a dove humbling, tranquilizing our inner most being, Our hearts, mind, body and soul.

Let freedom ring forevermore in your spirit that gives you power to praise God in the utmost high, as high as you can reach heaven's door gates.

God is Love, He is marvelous, a marvelous spirit. We must allow His Holy Spirit to manifest in us.
We, as Christians, do not let the Spirit of God, Our Father Jehovah, impart in us every day in our lives.
So, it's important that we discern in his word and never doubt his promises that will abide in us
if we obey and take heed to his commandments on a daily basis.

In those daily commandments we must walk and talk with the Lord Jesus Christ, Our Savior, the Son of God: Our Father which art in heaven, hallowed be Thy Name.

We must put our whole heart—not just a portion, but all of it—trust in Him that will deliver us from our sin sick soul.

Salvation is very vital in our lives. Hope in Jesus Christ is uplifting to your spirit. We are his concern.

God bless and keep you beneath His wings. Amen.
                    With God's Love

I am the Lord your God; walk in my statutes, and keep my judgements,
And do them; and hallow my Sabbaths; and they shall be a sign between me
And you, that ye may know that I am the Lord Your God.
Ezekiel 20: 19-20

I Come to Thee

I Come to Thee

I come to Thee, the Father

I come to Thee, in prayer

I come to Thee, in Jesus name

I come to Thee, in exaltation

I come to Thee, in supplication

I come to Thee, for I have sin and

come short to the glory of God

I come to Thee, for my redemption, to be set free

I come to Thee, for security

I come to Thee, for He is good

I come to Thee, to know that I have a mansion in heaven

I come to Thee, for this is the golden rule

I come to Thee, to give my soul, my mind and body

I come to Thee, the Father, Jehovah Jireh, in Jesus name

to have mercy upon my soul... Alleluia... Amen.

Alleluia

Alleluia

Inspired by the scripture Exodus 20:24 © 1999 by Charles Jones

GOD SEES AND KNOWS

God sees and knows our precious tender hearts and souls
Wherever you go and boast the word of God, Almighty God sees and knows
He plants the seeds of protection so no other can deceive our minds and souls
As we travel through the wilderness.
Have God first within a sincere heart, for this is the will of God
God sees and knows
Every day we are like sheep ready for slaughter
To be cast in hell damnation
At the same time we as followers, God's people
His protection blocks out pitfalls, stumbling blocks in roads and bridges
we must cross over daily.
God sees and knows
Long as God continues to see us through this land
He knows our trials and tribulations we face every day as his people.
God sees and knows
One thing for sure, according to his richest and blessings
You will make it into his sanctuary
A heaven he builds so we can call it home eternally
God sees and knows our tender hearts and souls
He cares, so dry your tear stained eyes
Have no fear in Him
Without his healing power you lose a very special gift God has to offer
Remember, God sees and knows.

In those days came John the Baptist, preaching in the wilderness of
Judaea, and saying, Repent ye: for the kingdom of heaven is at hand.
Matthew 3: 1-2

WHOSE SIDE ARE YOU ON?

Tell me, whose side are you on?
Tell me, can't you? Whose side are you on?
Please answer the question...

Sometimes we, as people on this green earth
We need to remind ourselves there is a God...
A powerful spirit upstairs
If you and I oneday...are going to walk up those golden stairs
We need to choose a side
God or the devil.
Be wise and choose the right path of righteousness.

Again, we, as people, need to remind ourselves to confess
the sin we share alone in our hearts and minds

Are we blinded by the world's pleasures of life?
We seek here, we seek there,
Yet getting nowhere in our lives.

There are too many people deceiving and mistreating
one another in high and low places
The devil is on the rise, he is moving at a fast pace.

If you choose the devil (Satan)
He can make you see things that appeared to be
As if God put it there for your fruitful well being
Don't be fooled and get swallowed up in Satan's web

It will make you wonder and say "whose side am I on?"
My friend, prepare your feet shod with the preparation of the gospel
of peace

"WHAT LOOKS GOOD
NOT ALWAYS GOD"

Satan has a plan bigger than your retirement residual
Long as you have God first, nothing can go wrong.
Make Him your everlasting throne.

Remember, God is powerful and enduring.

Beware of false prophets, which come to you in sheep's clothing,
But inwardly they are ravening wolves.
Matthew 7: 15

DEAR HEAVENLY FATHER

Dear Heavenly Father
Make me in thy own way to love again...
Dear Heavenly Father
Make me in thy own way to pray again...
To Thee I pray
With all sincerity from the heart
God, you are my blessing
Which all blessings flow day to day...
Gently the joy in my soul floods with happiness to call my own...
Your blood washes my sins white as snow...
Though at times I get weary,
Lord, you strengthen my soul.
Dear Heavenly Father
I pray to Thee
All this I ask in the name of Jesus Christ Our Savior. Amen.

YOU AND I AGAINST THE WIND

We've come thus far
to let the wind turn us around
from what we believe in.
That belief is God of Creation.

You and I against the wind
You and I against the wind
You and I against the wind.

Troubles will rise
Mountains roar
Wind will blow fiercely

Long as You and I against the wind
You never have to worry about a thing.

You and I against the wind
You and I against the wind
You and I against the wind.

Long as Jesus Christ, Our Savior, is always right there
To hold and comfort your heaviest burden
You will know and see that He cares.

Look to Him in troubled times
Look to Him in doubtful times
He shall surely amaze your heart's pleasure. Amen.

Thou art my hiding place;
thou shalt preserve me from
trouble; thou shalt compasse
me about with songs of
deliverance. Selah.
Psalms 32:7

SHAKE A HAND TO A HAND

Shake a hand Shake a hand
Shake a hand to a hand
to a hand...a hand
um umh...ah oop...shake a hand

Verse I
Show some kindness to your brother
Show him you care and respect his needs
So, won't you please shake his hand
and lead him to where God's holy word stands
And it sure to stand on promised land.

Shake a hand Shake a hand
Shake a hand to a hand
to a hand...a hand
um umh...ah oop...shake a hand.

Verse II
Show a smile and be of good courage
Shake a hand with a firm handshake to a hand
Cast out all that pride of yours
You don't need it, he can defeat it
It will bring you down
Be that sweet person with that good Godliness
inside of you
Why don't you shake a hand to a hand?

Bridge
Shake a hand Shake a hand
Shake a hand to a hand
Tell your neighbors to pass it along
to the other hand to a hand
Shake a hand to a hand
Shake a hand to a hand
Shake your father's hand
Shake your mother's hand
Shake your brother's hand
Shake your sister's hand to a hand
Children, grab a firm hand and shake it well.

COME HOME, MY DEAR CHILD

Come home, my dear child
Please come home Will you see about me
Come home... come on home.
You have a place in my heart
You gave me love when it seemed no one else cared.
You and only you can make it better.

When life for me got sadder
You came along and made it better
You are my dear child
My only dear child
Your smile comforts my pain and suffering
You are my light in the middle of the night.

I am glad to have you home, home by my side
It makes me want to cry knowing you're safe in my arms.
You came home to impart your time
to bond with me, your loved one.
I know I can always count on you
No matter what may come between us.
God must have sent you from up above
We as two can come together in love.

God, I thank you for my child's presence
You are my only child, the only child to see
and care about me.
You are my child. You are my child
My loving child. You are my child
My loving child

God brought you to me in my worst time of need
God sent your loving face
to heal my body and soul with laughter
To face my weakest days

You are like my amazing grace
I love you, my dear child.
I really do care for you, my child,
My only and only child
Thank you, God bless you, my child.

GOD MADE A WAY FOR ME

God made a way for me
No one can steal my joy away
Jesus instills it in me with all power in his hand
He shares his peace and love and joy with me
He shares it continuously.
I took heed to my Jesus' commandments
Then he reaches out towards me to take care of my every need.
I took hold of his healing hands
He lay me down and eased the pain
Now I thank God for his mercy and grace he blessed upon me
Jesus - He is my blessing assurance
My sins, he freely bears all of them.
It's because he cares for me indeed
It comforts me to know that God -
God made a way for me.
He loves me so that he gave to me the gift
Jesus Christ, the Son of God.
God gave his only begotten Son
to die on Calvary just for you and me
That we might have everlasting life forevermore.
Do not dare walk away from his word
His word which is ever true
It stands through the test of time.
Here on earth it is critical, for we need God
to make a way out of no way.
God made a way for me. He can do the same for you.
If you just believe in your heart and soul and
confess with your mouth and have faith.
He is coming back soon for the meek and lowly one
He is coming back for the church in heart and spirit
God made a way for me in his word that will never die
or depart eternity - God made a way for me.
My God made a way out of no way
God made a way for me
He can do the same for you.

Heal me, O Lord, and I
shall be healed; save me,
and I shall be saved: for
thou art my praise.
Jeremiah 17:14

PRECIOUS CHILD

I believe no one knows me.
They don't know who I am,
what I am to be in this world.

I believe everyone assumed they knew me,
what I am...or who I am to be in this world.

Inner child in me brings out the special side
that lives in me, in my soul to soul
Precious one...precious me...
I am God's precious child.

All the wrong I do in life shows me I'm only human.
It makes me proud and truly blessed
to know someone above is watching over me,
caring and sharing their love for me
As I am their precious child (hallelujah)
Precious child.

There is no way I can walk away from this feeling
I feel deep inside of me
knowing I am His precious child.

Lonesomeness and pain have been at my window pane
far and more distanced I face every day in the mirror
not knowing which way to turn - left or right
knowing I pause, I'm his precious child.
Knowing that, I walk a straight line to my destiny in time.

Inner me
The inner child
We're all God's precious children.
No matter what! No matter how! No matter where!

For God so loved the
world, that He gave His
only begotten son, that
whosoever believeth in
Him should not perish,
but have everlasting life.
John 3:16

BE STILL

Be still...
and know God's presence
Be still and know the gifts
God has bestowed upon you
for his mercy is great above all thing.

Be still...
and know the Holy Spirit
God allows to enter your soul
God is wonderful love
He is the lover of my soul

One place...
He will enter is the temple of your
body, mind and soul

Be still...
and know God's presence and be healed

Be still and know his anointed...
is real and comforting
Be of good courage and have a grateful heart
to God's blessings and his presence
be still and know God's way and understanding
to truth, to faith and his way.

Be still...
and know God's presence and be still, my child.

Inspired by Psalm 46

CAUGHT-UP (ROUND-UP IN A MESS)

CHORUS:

Don't get caught-up
    and round-up in a mess
Don't get caught-up
    and round-up in a mess

Steadfast and know he is God

All you do for the Lord with Christianity on your mind,
the spirit leads you intentionally to new life.

You pray and shout with your conviction in mind
in a dimensional place

Don't let it be insincere and double-minded

Vain glory is the abomination of God the Father, indeed

God is not pleased with the destruction of man caused upon himself
    using His name in vain with (heart and soul)

God is all and will be forevermore the same as yesterday

Take heed to his word
Ask forgiveness with a sincere prayer in Jesus Christ, the savior
For it is the right thing to do.

Spoken:
I discover this before I enter into a mess awaiting for me
It caught me by surprised...

KEEP YOUR CONSCIENCE CLEAR

Keep your conscience clear
    (when you pray)
Keep your conscience clear
    (when you pray)
Keep your conscience clear
    (when you pray)
Keep your conscience clear
    (when you fast)
Keep your conscience clear
    (when you fast)
Keep your conscience clear
    (when you fast)
Keep your conscience clear
    (when you fast)

LEAD:
Keep your conscience clear
    (when you fast and pray)
Keep your conscience clear
    (when you fast and pray)

LEAD VOCAL:
Lay aside all malice and all guile
and all hypocrisies and all envies
and all evil speaking
when you fast and pray
Keep your conscience clear at all time
for Jesus Christ is mine forevermore and more.

Meditate in spirit
Glorifying God in Jesus Christ
Keep a conscious clear mind
Praising the Savior in sincerity
Praising Him with a grateful heart.

Honor all men in Christ Jesus
Love they brotherhood
Fear God of gods
Honor the King of kings.

                                            (more)

Keep your conscience clear
Fear God, dearly beloved.
I say to you, don't be disobedient unto the
word of God through Jesus Christ, our Savior.

Keep a clear mind
Use your spiritual love affair
in wisdom to grow and manifest
In the holy word of God
For this is His foundation
for the few who come forth
with grace upon their faces.

Keep a clear mind and say:
Hallelujah, hallelujah, hallelujah
Hallelujah, hallelujah, hallelujah
With clear Mind I say:
Hallelujah, hallelujah, hallelujah
Hallelujah, hallelujah, hallelujah

This song of praise was inspired by 1 Peter 2
(the Holy Bible)

IN CASE YOU FORGOT
LET ME REMIND YOU . . .

You have a duty call beyond your being
Your Christian duties
Church we lose our power
Your Christian ways (Christ like)
We're not like what we used to be
We let the devil defeat on every end
We let him manifest himself in us
In case you forgot - let me remind you
You can destroy that old devil that has you bound in iniquity
Take hold of God's word and tell that old devil
Get thee behind me (Satan) I rebuke you
In the name of Jesus Christ the Lord
Obey God's law, the principle of God, Jehovah Jireh
Take heed to the church covenant
In case you forgot - let me remind you of something good
Be good to your neighbors
Be good to your elders
Be good to whosoever you meet in the street
Honor thy mother and thy father
Love thy brother and sister
In case you forgot - the world don't have to be on your shoulder
You can shake it off.

narrates:
In case you forgot - let me remind you
Whosoever love the Lord shall not perish
but have everlasting life
In case you forgot - let me remind you
If God be for us, who can separate us from the love of the Lord?
In case you forgot - let me remind you
For all things work together for good to them that love the Lord
and to them that are called according to his purpose. Amen
Hallelujah
Hallelujah
Hallelujah

Then said, Jesus unto his disciples, If any man will come
after me, let him deny himself, and take up his cross,
and follow me.
Matthew 16:24

Chapter 7
READ YOUR BIBLE

Encourage, Strengthen

Deuteronomy 3:28

But charge Joshua, and encourage him, and strengthen him: for he shall go over before this people, and he shall cause them to inherit the land which thou shalt see.

I Samuel 30:6

And David was greatly distressed; for the people spake of stoning him, because the soul of all the people was grieved, every man for his sons and his daughters: but David encouraged himself in the Lord his God.

Prosper, To Succeed

Psalms 1:3

And he shall be like a tree planted by the rivers of water, that bringeth forth his fruit in his season; his leaf also shall not wither, and whatsoever he doeth shall prosper.

Psalms 122:6

Pray for the peace of Jerusalem: they shall prosper that love thee.

Nehemiah 2:20

The God of heaven, he will prosper us; therefor we his servants will arise and build; but ye have no portion, not right, nor memorial, in Jerusalem.

3 John 2

Beloved, I wish above all things that thou mayest prosper and be in health, even as they soul prospereth.

SCRIPTURES MINISTRY

August 1998

Proverbs 27:20

Hell and destruction are never full; so the eyes of man are never satisfied.

Proverbs 30:16

The grave; and the barren womb; the earth that is not filled with water; and the fire that saith not, it is enough.

These scriptures was laid upon me during a church service
and it stuck to me like a hand in glove...

Chapter 8
THE SCRIPTURES

Jesus Teaches Forgiveness

St. Matthew 18: 20-22

For where two or three are gathered together in my name, there am I in the midst of them.
Then came Peter to him, and said, Lord, how oft shall my brother sin against me, and I forgive him? till seven times?
Jesus saith unto him, I say not unto thee, Until seven times: but, Until seventy times seven.

Mark 11:24

Therefore I say unto you, what things soever ye desire, when ye pray, believe that ye receive them, and ye shall have them.

Be Strong in the Lord

Ephesians 6:18-19

Praying always with all prayer and supplication in the spirit, and watching thereunto with all perseverance and supplication for all saints.
And for me, that utterance may be given unto me, that I may open my mouth boldly, to make known the mystery of the gospel.

Faith and Humility

James 1:19-21

Wherefore, my beloved brethren, let every man be swift to hear, slow to speak, slow to wrath;
For wrath of man worketh not the righteousness of God
Wherefore lay apart all filthiness and superfluity of naughtiness, and receive with meekness the engrafted word, which is able to save your souls.

These scriptures were given to me by my pastor.I had this notion to myself I would never tell or make mention of my problems to a preacher man. He's just a man. I prayed on it and confirmed with God. He touched my heart and made me whole. I stood still and knew that it was all right to go to my pastor, for spiritual advice. He is a man of God. I have great respect for him. I thank you, Lord Jesus. You are my regulator in times of pain and sorrow. Amen.

BE STRONG IN THE LORD

Ephesians 6: 10-18

Finally, my breathern, be strong in the Lord, and in the power of his might.
Put on the whole armour of God, that ye may be able to stand against the wiles of the devil.
For we wrestle not against flesh and blood, but against principalities, against powers, against the rulers of the darkness of this world, against spiritual wickedness in high places.
Wherefore take unto you the whole armour of God, that ye may be able to withstand in the evil day, and having done all, to stand.
Stand therefore, having your loins girt about with truth, and having on the breastplate of righteousness;
And your feet shod with the preparation of the gospel of peace;
Above all, taking the shield of faith, wherewith ye shall be able to quench all the fiery darts of the wicked.
And take the helmet of salvation, and the sword of the Spirit, which is the word of God:
Praying always with all prayer and supplication in the Spirit, and watching thereunto with all perseverance and supplication for all saints;

We need the armour, we need the armour, armour of the Lord
There is a war going on, and if you're going to win,
you got to put on a whole armour of God, power of God [1] Ψ

This scripture "Be Strong in the Lord" will protect inner soul, body and soul, heart and soul, my mind, spirit and soul from the devil of every attack he launches at me. Thank you, Jesus Christ, the Father, the Son of God. Amen

---

[1]   Samples from the song "There's a War Going On" by Walter L. Hawkins Ψ

PROPHECY OF THE PRINCE OF PEACE[2]

Isaiah 9:6

For unto us a child is born, unto us a son is given: and the government shall be upon his shoulder:
and his name shall be called Wonderful, Counselor, The mighty God, The everlasting Father, The Prince of Peace.

Isaiah 53:5

But he was wounded for our transgressions, he was bruised for our iniquities: the chastisement of our peace was upon him; and with his stripes we are healed.

Psalms 24:1 (A Psalm of David)

The earth is the Lord's, and the fullness thereof; the world, and they that dwell therein.

Psalm 35:1-2 (A Psalm of David)

Plead my cause, O Lord, with them that strive with me: fight against them that fight against me.
Take hold of shield and buckler, and stand up for mine help.

Psalms 23

The Lord is my shepherd; I shall not want.
He maketh me to lie down in green pastures; he leaded me beside the still waters.
He restoreth my soul: he leadeth me in the paths of righteousness for his name's sake.
Yea, though I walk through the valley of the shadow of death, I will fear no evil: for thou art with me, thy rod and they staff they comfort me.
Thou preparest a table before me in the presence of mine enemies: thou anointest my head with oil; my cup runneth over.
Surely goodness and mercy shall follow me all the days of my life: and I will dwell in the house of the Lord for ever.

---

[2]   Scripture given by Ken McCullough, December 1996

JEHOVAH IS MY STRENGTH

Jesus, the Messiah, Savior Our Lord

What I want the most is to give as much as I can to please the God Almighty, through the Lord, Jesus Christ.

What I don't know about Him, please give knowledge of His word that is so holy and majestic.

I will put my heart on the line to show the labor of love and strength; and endureth all strifes against me.

Lord Jesus, you are my Shepherd. Amen.

Charles Jones

Behold, God is my salvation; I will trust, and not be afraid:
For the Lord JEHOVAH is my strength and my songs;
he also is become my salvation.
Isaiah 12 : 2

Chapter 9
CHRISTIAN FREEDOM

Galatians 5:1

Stand fast therefore in the liberty wherewith Christ hath made us free, and be not entangled again with the yoke of bondage.

Galatians 6:3

For if a man think himself to be something, when he is nothing, he deceiveth himself.

Galatians 5:16-26

This I say then, Walk in the Spirit, and ye shall not fulfil the lust of the flesh.
For the flesh lusteth against the Spirit, and the Spirit against the flesh: and these are contrary the one to the other: so that ye cannot do the things ye would.
But if ye be led of the Spirit, ye are not under the law.
Now the works of the flesh are manifest, which are these; Adultery, fornication, uncleanness, lasciviousness,
Idolatry, witchcraft, hatred, variance, emulations, wrath, strife, seditions, heresies,
Envyings, murders, drunkenness, revellings, and such like: of the which I tell you before, as I have also told you in time past, that they which do such things shall not inherit the kingdom of God.
But the fruit of the Spirit is love, joy, peace, longsuffering, gentleness, goodness, faith,
Meekness, temperance: against such there is no law.
And they that are Christ's have crucified the flesh with the affections and lusts.
If we life in the Spirit, let us also walk in the Spirit.
Let us not be desirous of vain glory, provoking one another, envying one another.

CONCORDANCE

Bad words you don't want to live by (In Galatians)

Adultery - the act of voluntary sexual intercourse by a married person with someone other than his or her own spouse.

Fornication - illicit intercourse

Uncleanliness - not clean, sinful, unchaste

Lasciviousness - lustfulness

Idolatry - worship of idols

Witchcraft - the practice of magic

Hatred - the state of hating someone or something; hate

Variance - dissension; disagreeing, conflicting (of people) in a state of discord or enmity

Emulations - to try to do as well as or better than

Wrath - anger, indignation

Strife - quarreling, conflict

Seditions - riot; words or actions that make people rebel against the authority of the government

Heresies - unaccepted belief; a religious opinion that is contrary to the orthodox doctrine or accepted beliefs of a specific religion.

Envyings - to feel envy of someone or something

Murders - the intentional and unlawful killing of one person by another

Drunkenness - being intoxicated

Revelings - to take great delight, for example: some people revel in gossip

Good words to live by (In Galatians)

Kingdom of God - dominion of the King, that is God of Creation Heaven and Earth

Love - God benevolence toward mankind; warm liking or affection for a person

Joy - gladness

Peace - calm; repose

Longsuffering - bearing provocation patiently

Gentleness - kindness

Goodness - virtue; the quality of being good

Faith - reliance; belief in religious doctrine

Meekness - quiet and obedient, making no protest

Temperance - self-restraint in one's behavior or in eating and drinking.

These are clinical words used in the Bible. We, as people, should take heed and commend to God for this information; without it we are lost in ignorance.

Chapter 10
QUOTED SCRIPTURES

LORD, TEACH US TO PRAY

And it came to pass, that, as he was praying in a certain place, when he ceased, one of his disciples said unto him, Lord, teach us to pray as John also taught his disciples.

Unity in Christ

Romans 14:17

For the kingdom of God is not meat and drink; but righteousness, and peace, and joy in the Holy Ghost.

Romans 16:27

To God only wise, be glory through Jesus Christ forever. Amen.

Joshua's Words of Warning

Joshua 23:8

But cleave unto the Lord your God, as ye have done unto this day.

THE LORD'S PRAYER

Matthew 7:2

Judge not that ye be not judged for with what judgment ye judge, ye shall be judged: and with what measure ye mete it shall be measured to you again.

Matthew 6:9-13

After this manner therefore pray ye: Our Father which art in heaven, Hallowed be thy name.
Thy kingdom come. They will be done in earth, as it is in heaven.
Gife us this day our daily bread.
And forgive us our debts, as we forgive our debtors.
And lead us not into temptation, but deliver us from evil: For thine is the kingdom, and the power, and the glory, for ever. Amen.

A PRAYER TO GOD

Dear Lord,
I feel deprived in my soul.
Please help me to overcome the agonizing pain that I have suffered in life.
To those who do not care, show them the light and make their fellowship bright through your amplified power among all creeds, the afflicted, and all nationalities.
I pray on and on in your name, Lord, asking forgiveness by confession,
That my soul may be purified and my vision be focused on the light of your spirit.
Lord, also, freshen my tongue so that I may speak Your Name wisely.
Speak to me, Lord, in my ear so that I may perceive sounds and heed every command of your precious voice.
All this I ask in the name of Thy son, Jesus. Amen.

Charles

Isaiah 11:6

. . . and a little child shall lead them

CHRISTMAS DAY AT WORK

. . . learning to deal with life itself is bitter
with the sweet . . .

Two counts against you is all right
but three counts, you need to pray on your knees.
For the will of God through Jesus Christ is for real.
As you breathe the atmosphere of life,
Come on brother, try Jesus.
He is a friend indeed.
He is a surely goodness and mercy
that shall follow you the rest of your life.
Remember this.
God loves you and cares always forever.
Love Him back.

Charles Jones
December 25, 1996

Chapter 11
GOD IS THE JUDGE

The 51st Psalm in the Old Testament was a favorite to a dear friend Betty Jean Johnson aka Peaches. God has given her everlasting life now and forever, in the name of Jesus Christ. Love, Charles Jones

Psalms 51

Have mercy upon me, O God, according to thy loving kindness: according unto the multitude of thy tender mercies blot out my transgressions.
Wash me thoroughly from mine iniquity, and cleanse me from my sin.
For I acknowledge my transgressions: and my sin is ever before me.
Against thee, thee only, have I sinned, and done this evil in thy sight: that thou mightest be justified when thou speakest, and be clear when thou judgest.
Behold I was shapen in iniquity; and in sin did my mother conceive me.
Behold, thou desirest truth in the inward parts: and in the hidden part thou shalt make me to know wisdom.
Purge me with hyssop, and I shall be clean: wash me, and I shall be whiter than snow.
Make me to hear joy and gladness; that the bones which thou hast broken may rejoice.
Hide thy face from my sins, and blot out all mine iniquities.
Create in me a clean heart, O God; and renew a right spirit within me.
Cast me not away from thy presence; and take not thy holy spirit from me.
Restore unto me the joy of thy salvation; and uphold me with thy free spirit.
Then will I teach transgressors thy ways; and sinners shall be converted unto thee.
Deliver me from bloodguiltiness, O God, thou God of my salvation: and my tongue shall sing aloud of they righteousness.
O Lord, open thou my lips; and my mouth shall shew forth thy praise.
For thou desirest not sacrifice; else would I give it: thou delightest not in burnt offering.
The sacrifices of God are a broken spirit: a broken and a contrite heart, O God, thou wilt not despise.
Do good in thy good pleasure unto Zion: build thou the walls of Jerusalem.
Then shalt thou be pleased with the sacrifices of righteousness, with burnt offering and whole burnt offering: then shall they offer bullocks upon thine alter.

Isaiah 26:4

Trust ye in the Lord forever; for in the Lord Jehovah is everlasting strength.

Matthew 6:33

But seek ye first the kingdom of God, and His righteousness, and all these things shall be added unto you.

St. John 1:1

In the beginning was the Word, and the Word was with God, and the Word was God.

The Bread of Life

St. John 6:54-58

Whoso eateth my flesh, and drinketh my blood, hath eternal life; and I will raise him up at the last day.

For my flesh is meat indeed, and my flood is drink indeed.

He that eateth my flesh, and drinketh my blood, dwelleth in me, and I in him.

As the living Father hath sent me, and I live by the Father: so he that eateth me, even he shall live by me.

This is that bread which came down from heaven: not as your fathers did eat manna and are dead: he that eateth of this bread shall live for ever.

St. John 7:24

Judge not according to appearance, but judge righteous judgment.

Jesus Promises the Holy Spirit

St. John 14:1-6

Let not your heart be troubled: ye believe in God, believe also in me.

In my Father's house are many mansions: it if were not so, I would have told you. I go to prepare a place for you.

And if I go and prepare a place for you, I will come again, and receive you unto myself; that where I am, there ye may be also.

And whither I go ye know, and the way ye know.

Thomas saith unto him, Lord, we know not wither thou goest; and how can we know the way?

Jesus saith unto him, I am the way, the truth, and the life: no man cometh unto the Father, but by me.

You Are God's Temple

I Corinthians 3:16-17
Know ye not that ye are the temple of God, and that the spirit of God dwelleth in you?
If any man defile the temple of God, him shall God destroy; for the temple of God is holy which temple ye are.

Spiritual Gifts

I Corinthians 12:12-13
For as the body is one, and hath many members, and all the members of that one body, being many, are one body; so also is Christ.
For by one spirit are we all baptized into one body whether we be Jews or Gentiles, whether we be bond or free; and have been all made to drink into one spirit.

Paul Reaches Athens

Acts 17:24
God that made the world and all things therein, seeing that He is Lord of heaven and earth; dwelleth not in temples made with hands.

Ephesians 2:21 - Unity in Christ
In whom all the building fitly framed together groweth unto an holy temple in the Lord.

Separation From Unbelievers

II Corinthians 6:17-18
Wherefore come out from among them, and be ye separate, saith the Lord, and touch not the unclean thing and I will receive you and will be a Father unto you, and ye shall be my sons and daughters, saith the Lord almighty.

Jesus Heals A Blind Man

John 9:5
As long as I am in the world, I am the light of the world.

The Light Of The World

John 8:7
He that is without sin among you, let him first cast a stone at her.

The Bread of Life

John 6:50-51

This is the bread which cometh down from heaven, that a man eat thereof, and not die.
I am the living bread which came down from heaven; if any man eat of this bread, he shall live for ever; and the bread that I give is My flesh, which I will give for the life of the world.

More Than Conquerors

Romans 8:35-39
Who shall separate us from the love of Christ? Shall tribulation, or distress, or persecution, or famine, or nakedness, or peril, or sword?
As it is written For thy sake we are killed all the day long; we are accounted as sheep for the slaughter.
Nay, in all these things we are more than conquerors through him that loved us.
For I am persuaded, that neither death, nor life, nor angels, nor principalities, nor powers, nor things present nor things to come,
Nor height, nor depth, not any other creature, shall be able to separate us from the love of God, which is in Christ Jesus our Lord.

Romans 8:28
And we know that all things work together for good to them that love God, to them who are the called according to his purpose.

Romans 8:31-32
What shall we then say to these things? If God be for us, who can be against us?
He that spared not his own Son, but delivered him up for us all, how shall he not with him also freely give us all things?

These scriptures were written for us to take heed and follow unto God's word that will stand through the test of time. So read your Holy Bible daily and you will be a witness for the Lord. Amen.

LESSONS FOR DAILY LIFE

(Proverbs 6:16-23)

There are six things the Lord hates - no, seven things he detests:

1. haughty eyes
2. a lying tongue
3. hands that kill the innocent
4. a heart that plots evil
5. feet that race to do wrong
6. a false witness who pours out lies
7. a person who sows discord among brothers

My son, obey your father's commands, and don't neglect your mother's teaching. Keep their words always in your heart. Tie them around your neck. Wherever you walk, their counsel can lead you. When you sleep, they will protect you. When you wake up in the morning, they will advise you. For these commands and this teaching are a lamp to light the way ahead of you. The correction of Discipline is the way to life.

Transcribed

The Majesty of the Lord

But they that wait upon the Lord shall renew their strength; they shall mount up with wings as eagles; they shall run, and not faint.

(Isaiah 40:31)

The Steadfast Love of God

Delight thyself also in the Lord; and He shall give thee the desires of thine heart. Commit thy way unto the Lord; trust also in him; and he shall bring it to pass.

(Psalms 37:4-5)

Judge Not Others

Thou hypocrite, first cast out the beam out of thine own eye; and then shalt thou see clearly to cast out the mote out of they brother's eye.

(Matthew 7:5)

Seek, and Ye Shall Find

But seek ye first the kingdom of God, and his righteousness; and all these things shall be added unto you.

(Matthew 6:33)

The Transfiguration

And Jesus said unto them, Because of your unbelief: for verily I say unto you, If ye have faith as a grain of mustard seed, ye shall say unto this mountain, Remove hence to yonder place; and it shall remove; and nothing shall be impossible unto you.

(Matthew 17:20)

Flee from Idolatry

Whatsoever ye do, do all to the glory of God.

(I Corinthians 10:31)

My Light and My Salvation

The Lord is my light and my salvation; whom shall I fear? The Lord is the strength of my life; of whom shall I be afraid?

(Psalms 27:1)

Seek, and Ye Shall Find

Ask, and it shall be given you. Seek and ye shall find; Knock, and it shall be opened unto you For everyone that asketh receiveth; and he that seeketh findeth; and to him that knocketh it shall be opened.

(Matthew 7:7-8)

God So Loved the World
> For God so loved that world, that he gave his only begotten son that whosoever believeth in him should not perish, but have everlasting life.
>
> (John 3:16)

The Peace of God
> I can do all things through Christ which strengthen me.
>
> (Philippians 4:13)
>
> The grace of our Lord, Jesus Christ be with you all. Amen.
>
> (Philippians 4:23)

I had the privilege of reading The Power For Living. I came across some profound scriptures quoted from very successful athletes, who found Jesus as their personal Savior and Grace.

God bless the coming of the Holy Spirit.

Charles Jones
June, 1999

Draw Near With Faith

Not forsaking the assembling of ourselves together, as the manner of some is; but exhorting one another; and so much the more, as ye see the day approaching.

For if we sin wilfully after that we have received the knowledge of the truth, there remaineth no more sacrifice for sins.

(Hebrews 10:25-26)

This scriptures was given to me by a dear friend who intention are pure and discerning by the garce of God of love...God bless his soul eternally.

Charles Jones

Chapter 12
FASTING

If you are going to fast and pray, fast and pray in the name of Jesus Christ, Our Savior from which all blessings flow.

Isaiah 58:3-4

Wherefore have we fasted, say they, and thou seest not? Wherefore have we afflicted our soul, and thou takest no knowledge? Behold in the day of your fast ye find pleasure, and exact all your labours.
Behold, ye fast for strife and debate, and to smite with the fist of wickedness: ye shall not fast as ye do this day, to make your voice to be heard on high.

Matthew 6:16

Moreover when ye fast, be not, as the hypocrites, of a sad countenance: for they disfigure their faces, that they may appear unto men to fast. Verily I say unto you, They have their reward.

Luke 18:11-12

God, I thank thee, that I am not as other men are, extortioners, unjust, adulterers, or even as this publican.
I fast twice in the week, I give tithes of all that I possess.

We, as Christians in Jesus Christ Our Savior, ought to want to fast twice a week. It serves a purpose, and that purpose is to walk right, live right, talk right, pray right, think right and also, come correct unto God Almighty as you are. Once again, if you are thinking about fasting in His word, do it with all sincerity, seeking God's Holy word to fast and pray. Devour it during morning breakfast, afternoon lunch, evening dinner and good night bed snack. That's a bold hearty appetite to keep you going and spirit pressing on to that mark. I hope this is a blessing for you to stay strong in the Lord, Jesus Christ, Our Savior. Amen.

Sincerely yours,

Charles A. Jones
July 1999

Chapter 13
SPIRITUAL RELATIONSHIP

THE RELATIONSHIP I HAVE WITH JESUS

The relationship I have with Jesus is serious.
The relationship I have with Jesus Christ is rewarding.
He gave me a new life, after the old life I had before, you see.
You have to realize that Jesus loves you, and will never leave you.
If only you abide and obey in His word; and do the Master's will.
Nothing whatsoever can go wrong through His power of faith.
My relationship through the Lord, Jesus Christ, is serious.
It is nothing to play with.
So, relate yourself more openly to God in prayer.
But, you must take your prayer to Jesus Christ, the Son of God and
leave it there, and He will take it to the Master as plan in your favor.
What friend will go out of their way to do that for you? Tell me who?
Because heaven is a long way, I mean a long way up there,
and no one can walk up there and just do that for you,
but Jesus Christ the Savior, the Son of God.
Good Bye and may God deliver you in prayer.

I am the way, the truth, and the life: no man cometh
Unto the Father, but by me.
John 14: 6

DEAR HEAVENLY FATHER

Dear Heavenly Father,

I thank you so much, for my blessings. Lord, sometimes when I pray, I don't know what to say. My thoughts just disappear as if someone is interfering in my conversation between You and I.

Lord, I really do thank you for Jesus Christ. He has really been a true confidant in my daily walks. I can call on him when I need him. When I talk to him, he takes the time to hear me. One thing for sure, when I am confused about something, he gives me power and wisdom to read a scripture in the Bible. That's His way of making pure sense out of me.

I am on common ground with my Lord God, Through Jesus Christ, My Savior, My Keeper, My Redeemer, My Comforter. He is my Prince of Peace, My Counsel and My Healer. Most of all a true and considerate friend indeed.

I bless you, Lord, the Almighty Power in heaven and earth. Alleluia. Amen.

Sincerely, your child

Charles Anthony Jones

For unto us a child is born, unto us a son is given: and
the government shall be upon his shoulder: and his name
shall be called Wonderful, Counsellor, The mighty God,
The everlasting Father, The Prince of Peace.
Isaiah 9:6

DEAR LORD JESUS

I call on Jesus in despair and with desolation of my soul.
I pray to you to come and rescue my sin sick soul from destruction.
I have done wrong in my life.
I come to you for forgiveness.
I can't seem to run from this weariness that has me bonded in captivity.
My heart feels corrupt and incomplete.
I don't know how to love right because of all the plight in my way of living right.
Jesus, I can't, can't make it go away without your help.
My sins have taken me for a ride of destruction and beyond corruption.
Dear Heavenly Father, I almost lost my life
With every hurt and strife against me I couldn't seem to win this endless fight.
Day to day, night to night
I didn't give up because I believe in Jesus Christ.
Jesus was going to bring me out of darkness into a marvelous light.
I was gong to yell, "Victory, victory, victory to the God Almighty!"

One day, May 15, 1999, I pleaded to you:
Dear Lord Jesus, I utter your Holy name in prayer,
seeking the Kingdom of God first through the Son of God.
His name is Jesus Christ, Our Savior
He took away my doubts and fears, He cast me out of darkness
and drew me nearer to Thee.
He turned me around called my name "Charles Jones"
And spoke these words to me in ear: "I give you light of joy,
shield of faith." so I took heed to his words.
Now I can see my fulfillment of shield: faith, peace, joy and goodness
I need for the rest of my days and nights to come.

Violence shall no more be heard in thy land, wasting
nor destruction within thy borders; but thou shalt call thy
walls Salvation, and thy gates Praise.
Isaiah 60: 18

One Sunday I confessed to God of my sins in the name of Jesus Christ, Our Savior.
One coming Sunday I needed to testify from my heart because I was forgiven of my sins.
You see, I have faith and I believe in His word that will never fail.
"I will stand" on Judgment Day with no doubts.

Testify in the Lord Jesus Christ, Our Savior, for He is good

The late night clubs are not my life
You are really my life and strength
My lifestyle that has me bound in iniquities.
Change me, God, in Thy own way
to serve your Holy Name with authority.
Lord, you knew, I know what is right from
wrong I was raised that way.
I don't know why I hesitate the way I do.
Sometimes my desires get the best of me.
Knowing You insist in this world it just
won't get out of control. "My Sins."
Maybe I've learned to depend on you, Lord
You are letting me know who is who
and Almighty and powerful in this world.
I remember when I was sick in February of the year of '98,
My body was weak, my skin peeled like an apple and
I had a fever with temperature over 100 degrees.
It left me feeling dehydrated from that terrible illness.
"Lord," I said to myself, "please take me." I've been vile
and punishment was due, but, with the belief and faith
I have in you, Lord, I knew I was gonna come through
during this illness.
Lord, I won't lie to you, but I had some doubts in my
mind that I wasn't gonna make it.
Is that the natural part of being a human being?
Because you are in the business of changing lives.
Lord, I have a situation that's been pounding in
my head for sometime now.
Lord, whenever it comes (the change), let me
shine in the Holy Spirit that endureth forever.
For you are the way, the truth, and the way of life to live.
Stay with me, God, and forgive me in the name of
Jesus Christ, Our Savior. Amen. . . Alleluia

And besought him that they might only
touch the hem of his garment: and as many
touch we made perfectly whole
St. Matthew 14: 36

I PRAY

I pray
Lord, Have mercy upon me when I pray
I pray unto You, for You are worthy of praises
Teach me to pray, God, with the belief and
righteousness you grace upon my soul
I believe in Your Holy word forever . . .
I pray to you, God, Our Father, in Jesus' name
Believing You will deliver my goods and bread
of life to conquered heaven for a better home
to call my own . . .

Thank you, God, for Jesus Christ, Our Savior,
for His mercy and grace that rest
upon my mind, body and soul. Amen

The Lord is good unto them that wait for him, to
the soul that seeketh him.
Lamentations 3: 25

Give unto the Lord the glory due unto his name: bring
An offering, and come before him: worship the Lord in the
beauty of holiness.
I Chronicles 16: 29

SOMEDAY WE'LL MAKE IT

Someday we'll make it, if you and I,
Search into our hearts and find
the trust we buried in our hearts and mind.

Someday we'll make it, if you and I,
Leave the past behind us,
And God will set us free
in the midst of a thunderstorm bliss.

Someday we'll make it, if you and I,
Will taste and learn the sound,
The spirit you hear and see in the wind,
my friends. It's the answer to your problems,
If you've been seeking and searching.

Remember God is right there in your soul,
and remember Peace, Joy, Love and Happiness
is all you need. Amen

Therefore we are buried
with him by baptism into
death: that likes as Christ
was raised up from the
dead by the glory of the
Father, even so we also
should walk in newness of
life.
Romans 6: 4

MY LOVE IS . . .

My Love Is . . . kind and gentle as the cool summer breeze against the human flesh

My Love Is . . . strength from God that holds a family together when in turmoil

My Love Is . . . a powerful magnet that touches hearts that are broken in pieces

My Love Is . . . warm and remembered every Spring the month of April

My Love Is . . . love, true love, foundation love that a mother instills with compassion for the love toward her children

My Love Is . . . the kind of love from an individual who knows only the best of love

My Love Is . . .

My Love Is . . .

This poem came in to my mind when I needed someone to understand;
my love from within...to share, given to me from the Father above

LET IT GO, LET IT GO

There comes a time when you have
to put some things aside and let it go.

God is the key to your troubles.
When disturbed
Let it go, my friend, let it go
And your worries will become few
and the road is less dim.

When pain turns into fear,
pray to God and, surely,
He will come near.

Your pathway will be brighter
Your burdens will be lighter.
Leave it with the Lord
He will be your fighter.

Let it go, let it go.

When strife comes (let it go)
When billows roll (let it go)
When destruction is near (let it go)
and have no fear.

God is our refuge and strength, a very
present help in trouble.
Psalms 46 : 1

Chapter 14
℀SHOW COMPASSION FOR AIDS VICTIMS℀

You'll never know it could be you
or somebody you love so dearly... ℀

THOUGHTS FOR AIDS

A - means   Accomplishment
Don't let this disease put a stumbling block on your accomplishments
and achievements in the life we've shared

I - means   Improvement
Having this dreadful disease is not the end.
You have to keep on, keeping on proving yourself
to be better in sickness and wellness.

D - means   Discovery
This is truly a time to stop, look, listen and search for
discoveries within your heart you thought you never had.
It's there. Discover something special within you.
God put it there, especially if it's good and right.

S - means   Socializing
Let it be known; I will have a life through this tormenting disease
and after this tormenting disease.
People touch me, people hold me, people bond with me . . .
For heaven's sake, God's people love me . . .
Don't leave me out of social benefits and events. Please, have mercy on me

The mourning doves - Please bow your head to pray

This AIDS has caused a lot of grief and confusion in all walks of life
in this society we live and breath in.

People need people to pray and fight with sincere hearts to
conquer this AIDS we have endured.
We have praised among our human beings.
Let's find a cure and pray together for AIDS.

God blessed you!

Writer,
Charles Jones

RED RIBBON

Red ribbon, what does it mean? What does it symbolize?
Red ribbon, what is it for? What does it stand for near the test of times?
Red ribbon, what is its cause? Does it bring better understanding for a greater tomorrow?

So they say, "Red ribbon raised over billions of dollars for AIDS research, lab technology, public awareness, and clinical public use.

Who is stricken with the AIDS virus? Everyone looks at each other and quietly says, "not me."
scared out of their wits.

We need to educate the old and young, the awareness the Red Ribbon symbolizes
We're not saying it will bring a better or greater tomorrow, or cure.
We are saying beware the risk, for the risk is great in numbers to be
"Oh my!" children rich and poor are dying.

This dreadful disease knows nobody
nor Dad, nor Mom, little sister nor big brother
It knows no means of life or care
even the consistencies we share in life.

In my opinion, this deadly evil disease knows no boundaries
It destroys hopes and dreams all across the universe
Whether you're Black, White, Latin, Hispanic or Asian
It knows no color or gender.

So treat life with respect and with a lot of love, tenderness and grace
Take care of yourself.

(closing prayer with encouragement)

For our hope lies in God, only God our Father alone
through the Lord Jesus Christ our Savior
He can save us from danger and harm...Amen.

146

Chapter 15
HEARTFELT LETTERS

Dear Essence,

My family and I truly enjoy reading your magazine, which provides so much information to society and withstands the passing of time. The essence of your monthly journal has really given me peace of mind in knowing that my heritage still exists. It has given me a sense of pride and joy in my Father's work ethics, and the joy of love for my brothers' and sisters' pains and sorrows.

I know no other way to describe it. Your magazine shows me the true believers of the Lord, Jesus Christ, the Son of God. Essence Magazine reflects everything about us, whether we are black or white. It lets us know that we are not in this struggle alone; and we need to come together in unity and love, not divide ourselves in continents.

Let us join forces and become one world, one nation under God with liberty and justice for all. Pledge your life to Jesus and be saved, for the blood of Jesus is real. Praise Him, and read your Bible daily. Then you will be able to count your blessings one by one as they come.

May God bless you according to His will. Remember this, let the desires of your heart be unto the Lord Jesus, in prayer and in sincerity.

Love in Jesus Christ, the
Son of God, Heavenly Father

Charles A. Jones

A favorite scripture of mine to share:

Therefore I say unto you, what things so ever ye desire, when ye pray, believe that ye receive them, and ye shall have them.
Mark 11:24

Dear Gospel Today,

Congratulations on your tenth anniversary as America's Leading Christian Lifestyle Magazine!

You have been and always will be an inspiration in my life. Reading about the Lord God and Jesus Christ has put in my mind a bigger and more perspective picture of the relationship between God and myself.

I thank you for your input and your knowledge of what you write about, the anointed of God.

I would deeply appreciate your taking the time to read some inspirational literature, which I have enclosed, about God and what He has done for me. I have been writing gospel lyrics for many years and giving Him praises in many other ways through my writing.

Although I am not yet well known , and have not yet put out a CD with my spiritual poetry, I was wondering if you might do a write-up about me. Everything I do comes from the Lord God Almighty of heaven and earth. My talent goes directly to God in prayer.

I hope to hear from you at *Gospel Today* soon. Thank you.

Sincerely,

Charles A. Jones

Spoken: Our obedience must come from knowing that God is exactly who He says He is, not from a desire to get rewards.

quoted by In Touch Ministries

WORD OF PRAYER

A PRAYER TO GOD
FOR OUR CHILDREN
Next Generation

O Most High
We acknowledge
the gift and presence,
Which you bestow
upon our youth
in high and low
rich or poor
secret places upon the
spiritual and natural earth realm.
It is in your will
that every good and perfect gift
comes from the Lord
Jehovah that
our children are our precious
future
Born to win
In Jesus Name. Amen

CHARLES A. JONES

Fundraiser

To help needy children
in the near future...
A promise to keep

Remember This...

God loves everyone just the same.
Jesus said, "Suffer the little children
to come unto me... for of such is the
kingdom of God."

SUCCESS AT HAND
coming soon....

CHILDREN

Matthew 19:13-15, Mark 10:13-16, Luke 18:15-17

The childlike qualities of purity, enthusiasm and love received a divine blessing when Jesus said, "Suffer the little children to come unto me... for of such is the kingdom of God." When we express those same qualities, we too, receive a welcome into a kingdom of abundant happiness and peace.

"Children, obey your parents in all things; for this is well-pleasing unto the Lord.
Fathers provoke not your children to anger, lest they be discouraged."

Colossians 3:20,21

Ye are of God, little children, and have overcome them:
because greater is he that is in you, than he that is in the world.
I John 4 : 4

CHILDREN OF THE LORD

Then were there brought unto him little children, that he should put his hands on them, and pray and the disciples rebuked them.

But Jesus said, "Suffer little children, and forbid them not to come unto me; for such is the Kingdom of Heaven.

And he laid his hands on them, and departed thence.

And, behold, one came and said unto him, Good Master, what good thing shall I do, that I may have eternal life?

And he said unto him, Why callest thou me good? There is none good but one, that is God; but if thou wilt inter into life, keep the commandments.

He saith unto him, Which? Jesus said, Thou shalt do no murder, Thou shalt not commit adultery, Thou shalt not steal, Thou shalt not bear false witness. Honor thy father and thy mother; and, Thou shalt love thy neighbor as thyself.

The young man saith unto him, All these things have I kept from my youth up; what lack I yet?

Jesus said unto him, "If thou will be perfect, go and sell that thou hast and give to the poor, and thou shalt have treasure in heaven and come follow me."

But, when the young man heard that saying, he went away sorrowful for he had great possessions.

Then said Jesus unto his disciples, verily I say unto you, that a rich man shall hardly enter into the Kingdom of Heaven.

And again, I say unto you. It is easier for a camel to go through the eye of a needle, than a rich man to enter unto the Kingdom of God.

When his disciples heard it, they were exceedingly amazed, saying, Who then can be saved?

But Jesus beheld them, and said unto them, "With men this is impossible; but with God all things are possible.

All things are possible.
Children of the Lord.

KEEP THIS IN MIND AND SPIRIT

The good seed are the children of the kingdom
St. Matthew 13:38

Do we expect a new miracle for the next generation?
To break the curse of demons: the slavery of debts?
Do we expect a new manner of sense, of pride, of ignorance?
What do you do when a child is in agony and deprivation
that causes pain in the spirit, inability to function for a brighter future,
or to succeed in life expectancy though the future seems so far away?
To capture what truly belongs to them from the beginning,
before the foundation of the world?
Can they be persuaded to follow their dreams and visions
that are brought on by their innermost aspirations in sight of restoration?
We as mentors must show responsibility,
must show them the right way to God's pathway of righteousness.
And we must make sure to explain to them not to fall
for misleading, false imitations that life has to offer when in despair,
but to keep their heads up high and their bodies upright
in this land where in God we trust, under one nation.
When you need to have a conversation with children
who are in need of some attention and are beginning to grow in their teens,
teach the fundamental basics of life and the love of this
one holy man named Jesus who can save souls from the lake of fire.

Make it your desire to teach and nurture them through the bible or steer them
to bible study a place of refuge. (church)
That they might learn the true meaning of life; of true men and women of Christ.
That although one day they may come unto situations or circumstances
that they cannot handle, they will not have to bear them alone.
Then they will be able to watch, fight, and pray, and not lose their way,
but to meditate in spirit, to call on the Lord in faith that
the Lord will come running in troublesome times.
When young men and women, especially minority individuals, come to so many
odds,
they must know they should never walk alone through the rough seas without
faith,
but to keep their eyes on the Master with faith the size of a mustard seed,
for that is great faith for those who are measured by God, our Father.
To have insight that God can calm the stormy seas
when the water rises to the limit of drowning in gravitation.
As long as one is able to muster their faith, to conquer their fears and doubts
for a greater tomorrow filled with sunshine, they will have the power
to overcome any kind of adversity or emotional depression.
*To keep a praying spirit of love, meekness, good,
temperance, kindness, peace, joy, patience and faith.*
To stand tall in victory. Amen.
*Galatians 5:22

It has been an inspiration to write this in the midnight hour
with a concerning mind and spirit to bless whosoever might read this notation.

© 2005 by Charles Jones

155

Appendix I

Take time to read and indulged more of great poetry, lyrics, prayers and poems in all form and fashion. Likewise, the bible, hymnal, public library, website, spiritual media, secular media, local coffee café, and church seminars.

All My Favorites:

Books To Read 📚

The Holy Bible Old and New Testaments in the King James Version (KJV) by Thomas Nelson Inc.

His Passion Christ's Journey to the Resurrection ~Devotions for Every Day of the Year by Integrity Publishers

The Craft of Lyric Writing by Sheila Davis- Writer's Digest Books Publishers

With Skilful Hand The Story of King David by David T. Barnard- McGill-Queen's University Press

The Psalms of David by James S. Freemantle- HarperCollins Publishers

I Wonder As I Wander An Autobigraphical Journey by Langston Hughes- Thunder's Mouth Press

Songs of Wisdom by Jay David- William Morrow and Company

One Day My Soul Just Opened Up by Iyanla Vanzant- Simon & Schuster Publishers

Makes Me Wanna Holler A Young Black Man In America by Nathan McCall-Random House

Invisible Life A Novel E. Lynn Harris- Doubleday Dell

Eternal Victim Eternal Victor by Donnie McClurkin- Pneuma Life

Touching A Dead Man One Man's Explosive story of deliverance from homosexuality by DL Foster-Morris

The Bluest Eye Beloved Jazz by Toni Morrison- Quality Paperback Book Club

In The Spirit The Inspirational Writings by Susan L. Taylor- HarperCollins

The Color Purple by Alice Walker- Pocket Books

The Children's Hour by Lillian Hellman- Dramatists Play Service Inc.

I Know Why The Caged Bird Sings by Maya Angelou- Bantam Books

A Raisin In The Sun by Lorraine Hansberry- Vintage Books

The Language of Love Edited by Susan Polis Schutz Designed and Illustrated by Stephen Schutz- Blue Moutain Arts

Selected Poems by Gwendolyn Brooks- Harper & Row

Gwendolyn Brooks by Harry B. Shaw- Twayne

The Writer's Craft by John Hersey- Random House

Adam Clayton Powell, Jr. by Robert E. Jakoubek- Chelsea House

Langston Hughes by James A. Emanuel- Twayne

Contemporary Religious Poetry by Paul Ramsey- Paulist Press

Sons Of Freedom God & The Single Man by Gini Andrews- Zondervan Publishing House

Thurgood Marshall Warrior At The Bar, Rebel On The Bench by Michael D. Davis & Hunter R. Clarke- Carol Publishing Group

Hair Story Untangling The Roots Of Black Hair In America by Ayana D. Byrd & Lori L. Tharps- St. Martin

Web sites: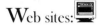

Aol blackvoices

✡ International Fellowship of Christians and Jews...log on to www.ifcj.org
Bible Gateway
Songwritersuniverse
Blackgospel.com –Black Gospel Music Clef- Your Music Ministries
TurningPoint Ministries
Coral Ridge Hour
Harvest Ministries
The Dream Center
Babbie Mason
The American Society of Composers, Authors and Publishers
The Maker's Diet
The Word Network
Zoe Ministries
The Potter's House
Juanita Bynum Ministries
The King is Coming
Oprah
Essence
Writer's Journal
TBN
Gospel Music
Love Center Ministries, Inc.
GTM Gospel Truth Magazine
Gospel City
G-Zone
In Touch Ministries
Sound and Spirit
Black Entertainment
BET
The Benefit Network
Jewish Voice Ministries International Magazine
Witnessfortheworld
Mybrotha
The Art of Poetry Enlivened
The Thunderbolth
The Light of the World: Poetic Imagery and the Gospel
HUM Health Unlimited Ministries~ Hope-Healing-Health
Gospelflava
The New Life Changers International Church
GospelToday
CTN Christian Television Network

UGA Urban Gospel Alliance~Those Who Bring Light To The Streets
Streaming Faith
Welcome to Blessed Herbs
Paula White Ministries
Ebony / Jet Magazine
John F. Germany Library

This is great to know the level of resources you can acquire from surfing the internet. Living in these ages a person's thoughts are ingenious and alto generate a very important message from the real sources of life—(God Almighty) to share what we encounter as human in our daily lives. God bless.

Charles

Sometimes the lyrics we listen to can take us on a high. As we wander through the wilderness in our flesh and spirit until we reach the Promise land...so be it.

Music is a powerful tool...

Charles

Appendix II

Genre of Music: (Gospel, Urban, Christian Pop/Rock , Southern Gospel, Classical, R&B Soul, Rap, Latin, Black Gospel, Reggae, Jazz, Alternative, Opera, Folks, House Blues, Spoken, Hip Hop, Word and Country)

The Philippians
Walter Hawkins and the Love Center Choir
Edwin Hawkins and the Edwin Hawkins Singers
Tramaine Hawkins
The Clark Sisters
Karen Clark Sheard
Dorinda Clark Cole
Twinkie Clark
The Potter's House Mass Choir
Donald Lawrence & The Tri-City Singers
John P. Kee
Debra Killings
Bobby Jones & New Life
Donnie McClurkin
Mary Mary
Ann Nesby
The Caravans
Inez Andrews
Shirley Caesar
JoAnn Rosario
Albertina Walker
James Cleveland
Aretha Franklin
Israel and New Breed
Byron Cage
Kurt Carr Singers
Chicago Mass Choir
The Christianaires
The Canton Spirituals
Daryl Coley
Comissioned
The Soul Stirrers
Andrae`Crouch
Yolanda Adams
Fred Hammond
Deleon
Helen Baylor
Vanessa Bell Armstrong
Anointed
CeCe Winans

Carol Bayer Sager
Christopher Williams
Patti Austin
En Vogue
Trey Lorenze
Regina Belle
Mikki Howard
Billy Ocean
Chante Moore
Keith Washington
Madonna
Boy George
Ru Paul
Syvester
Gladys Knight
Carla Simmon
Norah Jones
Larmar Campbell
Al Green
Toni Braxton
Natalie Cole
Nat King Cole
Tracy Chapman
Phil Collins
Fantasia
Ruben Studdard
Randy Crawford
Common
Lenny Kravitz
Clay Aiken
Lynette Hawkins
Mighty Clouds of Joy
Ben Tankard
Percy Bady
Staple Singers
B. B. King
Beverly Crawford
Etta Jones
Lena Horne

Appendix III

BeBe Winans
The Winans
Kirk Franklin
Georgia Mass Choir
Lashell Griffin
Deitrick Hadden
Mahalia Jackson
Dottie People
Lashun Pace
Richard Smallwood & Smallwood Singers
50 cent
The Very Best of Rev. James Moore
Trin-I-Tee 5:7
Tonex
Hezekiah Walker
Smokie Norful
Evelyn Turrentine-Agee
Virtue
The Williams Brothers
The Goodman
The Third Day
Randy Travis
Glenn Campbell
Carman
DC Talk
Dead Poetic
Shirley Murdock
Amy Grant
Grits
Point of Grace
Nicole C. Mullen
Sandi Patty
Out Of Eden
Michael W. Smith
Alvin Slaughter
Smalltown Poets
Rebecca St. James
Marvin Gaye
Luther Vandross
Diana Ross
Whitney Houston
Alicia Keys
Lionel Richie
Tina Turner

Josephine Baker
Sarah Vaughan
Barry White
Otis Redding
Bobby Bland
Etta James
Dinah Washington
Rosemary Clooney
LaVern Baker
Johnnie Taylor
Isaac Hayes
Babyface
Ashford & Simpson
Aaron Neville
The O'Jays
Teddy Pendergrass
Carly Simon
Bee Gees
John Denver
Dinah Shore
Connie Francis
Judy Garland
Christopher Cross
Carol King
Santana
Burt Bachrach
Four Tops
Sammy Davis
Bing Crosby
Ella Fritzgerald
Bessie Smith
Pearl Bailey
Duke Ellington
Eubie Blake
Donna Summers
The Pointer Sisters
Cissy Houston
The Gap Band
Atlantic Starr
Tevin Campbell
Cool and the Gang
The Beatles
Clara Ward
Peaches & Herb

Appendix IV

The Essential Simon & Garfunkel
Angie Stone
The Miracles
Jackie Wilson
LL Cool J
Anita Baker
Elvis Presley
Mario
Mary J Blige
Will Downing
Maxwell
Musiq
Kelly Price
Mariah Carey
Jennifer Holliday
Oleta Adams
Phyllis Hyman
Sade
Kenny G
Kirk Whalum
Patti Labelle
Chaka Kahn
Ray Charles
Little Richard
Stevie Wonder
Stephanie Mills
The Jackson Five
Donny & Marie Osmond
Nancy Wilson
The Whispers
Minnie Rippenton
The Emotion
The Jones Girls
Loretta Lynn
Barbara Mandrell
Dolly Parton
Trisha Yearwood
Ann Murray
Prince
Billie Holiday
The Isley Brothers
Earth,Wind,& Fire
Jeffrey Osborne
Joan Baez

Sean Paul
Shaggy
Wayne Wonder
Ludwig van Beethoven
Wolfgang Amadeus Mozart
Johann Sebastian Bach
Tony Bennet
Pat Boone
Perry Como
Paul Anka
George Michael
Vesta
Me'lisa Morgan
Jean Carne
Darlene Love
Usher
Candi Staton
The Delfonics
Cheryl Lynn
Shanice Wilson
Brandy
Monica
India Arie
Isley Jasper
Kenny Lattimore
Teena Marie
Destiny's Child
Eagles
Rachelle Ferrell
Johnny Gill
Bob Dylan
Curtis Mayfield
Willie Nelson
Bonnie Raitt
Linda Ronstadt
Avril Lavigne
Glenn Lewis
Mos Def
Lee Greenwood
Freddie Jackson
Captain & Tennille
Erykah Badu
Count Bessie
Al Jarreau

Appendix V

Joe Cocker
Peabo Bryson
Neil Diamond
Quincy Jones
Carpenters
Roberta Flack
Barbara Streisand
Elton John
Bob Marley
Ziggy Marley
John Lennon
The Mamas and The Papas
Bruce Springsteen
The Platters
Rickie Martin
Marc Anthony
Keith Lockhart
Leontyne Price
Kathleen Battle
Denyce Graves
Marion Anderson
Vicki Winans
Cassandra Wilson
Diane Krall
Jonathan Butler
Ricky Fante
Joe
Michel Camilo
Run DMC
The Florida Orchestra
Kierra KiKi Sheard
Sister Rosetta Tharp
Dr. Thomas Dorsey
Sallie Martin
Howard Hewitt
Barry Manilow
Neil Sedaka
Bette Midler
Celine Dion
Gloria Estefan
Seal
Cab Calloway
Esther Phillips
Frank Sinatra

George Benson
Denice Williams
Marvin Sapp
Jessie Dixon
Sounds of Blackness
Nightingales
Tata Vega
Five Blind Boys
Sister Sledge
Angela Winbush
Carlton Pearson
The Florida Mass Choir
Mississippi Mass Choir
Chicago Mass Choir
Dorothy Love Coates
The Barrett Sisters
Julio Iglesias, Jr.
Enrigue Iglesias
Hall & Oates
Jamie Foxx
Rolling Stones
Boyz II Men
Garth Brooks
Jimmy Buffett
Faith Evans
Jay-Z
Alanis Morissette
Jewel
The Roots
Jill Scott
Sting
Take 6
Luis Miguel
Orlando Lopez
2 Pac
Luciano Pavarotti
Wyclef
Michael Jackson
Public Enemy
Dr. Dre
Rita Dove
Ethel Waters
Earth Kitt
Sinead O Connor

Appendix VI

The best songwriters that have ever walked the planet

Here's a list of some of the greatest songwriters of the last 50 years. Their work will continue to inspire others for years to come. Maybe you too can find some inspiration from their songwriting success.

List of greatest songwriters:

Alan Bergman	Eric Clapton	Marvin Hamlisch
Antoine "fats" Domino Jr.	Felice Bryant	Maurice Gibb
Antonio Carlos Jobim	Fred Ebb	Michael Jackson
Barry Gibb	Gerry Goffin	Michael Legrand
Barry Manilow	Glenn Frey	Mick Jagger
Barry Mann	Hal David	Mike Stoller
Bernie Taupin	Harlan Howard	Miss Peggy Lee
Billy Joel	Howard Greenfield	Mort Shuman
Bob Merrill	James Brown	Neil Diamond
Bobby Darin	James Taylor	Neil Sedaka
Boudleaux Bryant	Jeff Barry	Nickolas Ashford
Bob Crewe	Jerome "Doc" Pomus	Norman Gimbel
Bob Dylan	Jerry Block	Otis Blackwell
Bob Gaudio	Jerry Herman	Otis Redding
Bob Hilliard	Jerry Leiber	Paul Anka
Brian Wilson	Jerry Ross	Paul McCartney
Bruce Springsteen	Jim Croce	Paul Simon
Buddy Holly	Jimmy Webb	Paul Williams
Burt Bacharach	John Barry	Phil Collins
Carly Simon	John Denver	Phil Spector
Carole King	John Kander	Queen
Carole Bayer Sager	John Lennon	Randy Newman
Carolyn Leigh	John Williams	Richard Adler
Charles Aznavour	Joni Mitchell	Robin Gibb
Charles Strouse	Keith Richards	Roy Orbison
Chuck Berry	Kenneth Gamble	Sheldon Harnick
Curtis Mayfield	Kris Kristofferson	Sir Andrews Lloyd Webber
Cynthia Weil	Lamont Dozier	Sir Elton John
Dave Bartholomew	Lee Adams	Sir Tim Rice
Diane Warren	Leon Huff	Smokey Robinson
Dolly Parton	Linda Creed	Stephen Sondheim
Don Henly	Lionel Richie	Stevie Wonder
Edward Holland	Little Richard	Sting
Ellie Greenwich	Marilyn Bergman	Valerie Simpson

Appendix VI

Walter L. Hawkins
Willie Nelson
Andre Crouch
Sandra Couch
Kevin Bond
Donald Lawrence
Tonex
John P. Kee
Ray Charles
Thomas Dorsey
Mariah Carey
Patricia Rushen
Quincy Jones
Melissa Etheridge
Edwin R. Hawkins
Dottie Rambo
Charles A. Jones
R. Kelly
Carlos Santana

Study the work of some of these great song writers and see how you
can apply various techniques and strategies to your songwriting.

Go to www.UltimateSongwriting.com *by permission*

EPILOGUE

There are times we need help in our everyday lives with health insurance, medical expenses, education, housing for low income families, domestic violence, child abuse, world catastrophe, etc. There are organizations that are willing to help all over the world. If you just purchased this book and found that it was interesting to read, and it has given you the strength in your faith to press forward in your belief in God. Make a contribution to one of these non-profit organizations listed below, I have and it's indeed rewarding to the holy spirit. There is a scripture that God loves a cheerful giver in 2 Corinthians 9:7 Every man according as he purposeth in his heart, so let him give; not grudgingly, or of necessity: for God loveth a cheerful giver. kjv

Contribution: These organizations and their Web sites are listed below:

The Dream Center
Attn: Development
PO Box 26629
Los Angeles, CA 90026
www.dreamcenter.org or
info@dreamcenter.org

Samaritan's Purse International Relief
PO Box 3000
Boone, NC 28607
www.samaritanpurse.org or
1-800-353-5959

Web Giving
American Foundation for AIDS Research
120 Wall Street
13th Floor
New York, NY 10005-3902
www.AmfAR.org
(212) 806-1600 tel.
(212) 802-1601 fax.

Gulf Coast Jewish Family Services
Development Department
14041 Icot Blvd.
Clearwater, FL 33760
www.tampaaidsnetwork.org or
info@gcjfs.org
1-800-888-5066 ext. 3060

American Cancer Society, Attn: Web
PO Box 102454
Atlanta, GA 30368-2454
www.acs.org or 1-800-ACS-2345

For memorials and honorariums

Americans Diabetes Association
PO Box 1131
Fairfax, VA 22038-1131
www.diabetes.org or
general donation
American Diabetes Association- Web
PO Box 7023
Merrifield, VA 22116-7023
by phone 1-800-DIABETES

Metropolitan Ministries
2002 North Florida Ave.
Tampa, FL 33602
www.metromin.org or
(813) 209-1022

The Fortune Society
53 West 23rd Street
8th Floor
New York, NY 10010
www.fortunesociet.org or contact
Brian Robinson @ (212)691-7554 ext. 526

727-538-7150 ext. 3060

To find out about HIV/AIDS resources in your local area,
call the COC National AIDS Hotline at 1-800-342-2437

United Negro College Fund
Attn: Accounts Receivable
8260 Willow Oaks Corporate Drive
PO Box 10444
Fairfax, VA 22031-8006

www.uncf.org or 1-800-331-2244

Big Brothers Big Sisters
www.bbsa.org

Boys & Girls Club of America
www.bgca.org

The Salvation Army
www.1salvationarmy.org

The Film Music Society
www.thefilmsociety.org

American Heart Association
www.heart.org

American Public Health Association
www.apha.org

Save Africa's Children
Post Office Box 8386
Los Angeles, CA 90008
www.saveafricaschildren.com
contact us online, 24 hours a day- 7 days
a week, or by phone, fax or u.s. mail
email address info@saveafricaschildren.org
phone 1(323) 733-1048 or toll-free
1-(866)313-2722
fax 1(323) 735-1141

Chronic Disease Directors
www.chronicdisease.org

Help to provide for the Jews in Israel
www.wingsofeagles.tv

Cure Autism Now
    Walk now
www.walknow.org

Value
Your Positive Thoughts
In Your Mind
And By All Means
Treasure The Possibilities
In Life

☞Quotation by Charles Jones
Inspired by Psalm 139:17,23 Deuteronomy 28:12

168

☎ PHONE SERVICES FOR THE HELP...
The presence of God in calamity

God is our refuge and strength, a very present help in trouble
Psalm 46:1

There are helpful phone numbers available for information throughout this country; to be of service to whoever is in need or just visiting the Tampa Bay Area, Florida Keys. Remember, the State of Florida offers the best in service.

AIDS Hotline	(800) 352-2437
Alzheimer's Disease	
And Related Disorders	(800) 621-0379
American Heart Association	(800) 242-8721
Bay Area Legal Services	(813) 232-1343
Cancer Information Center	(800) 422-6237
Child Support/Enforcement	(800) 622-5437
Child/Adult Abuse Hotline	(800) 962-2873
Consumer Service (Complaints)	(800) 435-7352
Department of Insurance	(800) 342-2762
Department of Revenue	(800) 352-3671
Elder Helpline	(800) 262-2243
Florida Emergency	
Information Line	(800) 342-3557
Florida Parks and Recreation	(850) 488-9872
Florida Poison Information Center	(800) 222-1222
Immigration	(800) 375-5283
Medicare Claims	(800) 333-7586
Public Service Commission	(800) 342-3552
Social Security	(800) 772-1213
Tampa Bay Workforce Alliance, Inc.	(813) 740-4680
Veterans Information	(800) 827-1000
Visit Florida	(888) 535-2872
Workers Compensation	(800) 342-1741

My nature is all about helping people in need of sheltering and boarding...God will take care of you...I know He will...yes He will... God will...Bless you!-my brothers and sisters-

Notes:

Confess your faults one to another, and pray one for
another, that ye may be healed. The effectual fervent
prayer of a righteous man availeth much.
James 5:16

This book is Dedicated In Memory of
Families and Dear Friends
who have gone on to be with the Lord

Grandfather Anthony Myers
Deceased
Grandmother Pauline S. Myers
Deceased
Uncle Willie Stanley
Deceased
Cousin Eliza Weathers
November 12, 1910 – November 20, 1996
Cousin Ruthalee Bradshaw Holmes
August 9, 1929 – October 11, 1996
Uncle Buster
February 11, 1909 – April 29, 1999
Cousin Maude McGee
Deceased
Cousin Stella Chambers
May 9, 1914 – February 11, 1985
Cousin Ramon J. Bradshaw, Sr.
October 31, 1969 – April 19, 1989
Uncle Paul A. Myers
Deceased 1994
Uncle John Myers
Deceased 2005
Zella May Myers
May 30, 1930 – April 4, 1996
Rosetine Russell
July 22, 1954 – May 20, 2003
Mary Juanita Bell
1946 – 1985
Fannie Lee Webster
May 31, 1922 – September 13, 2003
Sister Aslen Olive Gilley
December 25, 1914 – May 25, 2002
Sister Catherine Farragut
Deceased
Deacon Eugene Clarke
Deceased
Steven Velez
June 28, 1966 – April 15, 2000

Melvin Hair
August 20, 1963 – February 18, 1987
Rev. T. J. James
June 9, 1916 – May 26, 1991
Rev. Harvey Nichols
Deceased
Miss Rose Williamson
Deceased
Mrs. Lillian Pride
Deceased
Mrs. Odom
Deceased
Mrs. Agnes Barnes
Deceased
Mrs. Freeman
Deceased
Shirley McQuire
Deceased 2002
Kenny Hart
Deceased
Doretha Johnson
Deceased
Valerie "Penny" Johnson
Deceased
Betty " Peaches" Johnson
Deceased
Mrs. Valita Valdez
Deceased
Barbara Ann Bell "Bobby"
October 18, 1932 – February 9, 1993
Hazel Nelson Jones
July 1, 1933 - August 2, 2005
Carrie Lou House
Deceased
Alfred Alexander
Deceased

Special praise and appreciation to
God, Our Creator, who sent his only begotten son to die on Calvary
For our sins
To all who contributed to this **_Labor_** of **_Love_**
This book of poetry, song and prayers is also dedicated
To my nices and nephews who have enlisted my days and nights
Thank you, for you in Jesus Christ ...

From: MTA
To: Charles Jones
Subject: Re: Homosexuality Question
Date: Sat, 02 Jul 2005 09:18 :06 -0700

Charles Jones wrote:

What I am about to say," to pray for me to stay strong in the Lord, Christ Jesus

As I am going through healing living in a homosexual relationship, I want to end this relationship; I've come to know in my heart and especially in my mind that it is abomination to the Father I served. I will in my continuance to live my life in obedience unto God. I have a book coming out in the mid-fall-I must line-up and focus with the book I wrote to serve a purposed to recruit soul for the armor of the Lord. I will try to keep in mind that I can't worry about what people will say about my past...

Hello Charles

Thank you for your email. I am Praying for you.

I apologize for the delay in answering.

What you are doing is glorifying God. Only those who turn their backs on God will talk about your past in a negative way. Those who love the Lord will see the great work the Lord has done in your life and praise Him for it.

Thank you for your email. It is encouraging to us to hear about your walk with the Lord. Please stay in touch and let me know how you are doing and how the Lord is working in your life

Yours in the Love of Christ,
Steve
Mission to America

The sudden coming of the Lord

Are you going to be ready when Jesus come?
The living son, lets get caught up together

1 Thessalonians 4: 13-18

Re: One Day

⌨ To: Lora Johnson
cc:
Subject: One Day ⬚
Date: 04/04/01 09:22 AM

Lora-

One day you will come around to see for what God is really about. Not in a sense of emotional feeling-that will be the Holy Spirit job. This world is to big for a Christian to center in one place. You must spread the gospel where He see fit for the unfit. One thing I've learned about God is no matter how low I get in life, I can rest assured He will never leave nor forsake me because- He's That Kind Of A Friend that stick closer than a brother. You can even count on Him through many danger toils and snares. I will never grow old in His presence. Count on that, for He is right and good… there's a favorite old hymnal song; I keep in my heart to sing to my Father when I am at my lowest.

Blessed Assurance, Jesus Is Mine

Blessed assurance, Jesus is mine! O what a foretaste of
Glory divine! Heir of salvation, purchase of God,
Born of His spirit, washed in His Blood

This is my story, this is my song, Praising my Savior all the day long.
This is my story, this is my song, Praising my Savior all the day long.

Perfect submission, all is at rest; I in my Savior am happy and blest, Watching and waiting
looking above, Filled with His goodness, lost in His love

This is my story, this is my song, Praising my Savior all the day long
This is my story, this is my song, Praising my Savior all the day long

Words: Fanny J. Crosby, 1820-1915
Tune: Phoebe P. Knapp, 1839-1908

cc:
Subject: Re: One Day 🗁
Date: 04/04/01 10:02 AM

Charles,

There is scriptural reference (in the book of Acts) that born again believers were called Christians. Christian mean one who is Christ like. If you study and read the bible as you claim you do (smile) the bible says that we are not to be unequally yoke with unbelievers. Now if God called you go specifically into the bars and clubs to witness to the lost, by all means you better go. For it is better to obey God then man. However, you better make sure that God has instructed you.

Regarding leadership. Leadership is biblical – "Obey those that have rule over you for they watch out for your soul." Do not forake the assembling of yourselves – meaning that we Christians need fellowship with other believers in an environment that motivates and encourage one another. The Pastor is call into the 5-fold minister the word of God to you, To build you up until we all come together in one faith (Eph. 4).

I was born again at age of 19 or 20 years of age. I still did "wordly" things because my mind was not renewed. For years I did not know "who" I was in Christ and my authority as a believer. Mostly due to traditional teaching and not reading and studing for myself.

But now, after all the mistakes I made in my past, bad choices and decisions, everything have been washed in the blood of Christ. There is no condemnation nor guilt. My life is now hidden in Christ. I am a new creation. What I am saying is that it does not matter what you have done in your past. Once you have accepted Christ as your savior, the Holy Spirit comes to live on the inside of you. God does not see Charles and all his flaws, he sees Jesus Christ – his son.

There are many people confess that they are born again (i.e. Christians) and the life they live does not line up with there confession. However, when they renew their minds (change their thinking about themselves) and see themselves as God sees them, they would not do the things they do and behave the way they do.

I don't condemned no man, but I have to say what the Lord places on my heart to say. You and I were already condemned before God sent his son, Jesus to die for our sins. And it is so true that God loves mankind but because of sin, he can not do the things he want to do for them. Sin is like a wall which blocks the way to God. Remember when Jesus was on the cross an he cried " My God, My God – why has thou forsake me.?"
It was there Jesus became sin and knowing that God can not look at sin, he turn his back. Not on Jesus, but on sin.

Sin came in through Adam's disobedience to God and his submissiveness to Satan. Righteousness came in through Jesus's obedience to God and his submissiveness to God. If you are born again, you are the righteousness of God through Christ Jesus.

Tampan Shares His Musical And Written Talents With Others

BY IRIS B. HOLTON
Sentinel Staff Writer

Oftentimes, as young children, attending church services is just as much a part of our lives as breathing. However, after we reach the age of maturity and make our own decisions, we drift away from our upbringing.

But if the old adage that "a leaf doesn't fall far from the tree," is true, then eventually most people return to what has been a part of their early lives. **Charles Jones** describes himself as "raised in the church. I strayed away from the Word, but God never left me," he said.

A decade passed before **Jones** returned to his religious upbringing, but he's totally committed. The young man stated now he uses his talent as a writer to work for God.

He does this through writing prayers and gospel songs that he willingly shares with others. He discovered his special gift for writing as a teenager. And, with the passage of time, he has continued to write.

However, his talents are not limited to his ability to place words on paper in prose form. He says of the

CHARLES JONES
Aspiring Writer

songs he's created, "my gospel has not left the Word. Some people choose not to use the words God or Jesus. But the Bible is still the same."

He categorizes his music as "gospel music that is contemporary, but in a traditional package." He also sings and has been a member of the Edwin Hawkins Music and Arts Seminar since 1983. The organization hosts week-long training sessions in the areas of vocal techniques, song writing, sacred dance, music lessons, gospel business, copyright deals, and other aspects of the gospel arena.

But **Jones** gives all credit for his abilities to God and says, "He allows you to share what you're doing for Him with others." In keeping with that theory, **Jones** has printed bookmarkers with an original prayer printed on it that he passes out to people he meets. He shares this prayer with strangers walking down the street, at the Salvation Army, or Metropolitan Ministries.

But he is quick to point out that all one has to do is read the Bible because there are so many prayers in the Bible. However, he cautions that one should know how to pray.

It stands to reason that music would always be intertwined with his life. He is one of four children born to **Mrs. Annie Myers Jones,** a retired music teacher, who he credits with being his earthly inspiration.

At the age of thirty-two, he hopes to embark upon a career as a gospel songwriter. In the meantime, he is in the process of renewing his membership with the church of his childhood, Mt. Tabor M. B. Church, visiting other churches in the community, and sharing his gift with others.

∝Coping∝

It takes a basket of nerves to cope with a situation; that *you-yourself* sometimes
have no control over.
Especially, if its someone else's problem…
When dealing with other people's curse and battles-
Still, in the *midst* of it all God will continue to keep you
as His own…
God has made His yoke easy;
Therefore, when I decided to accept Jesus as my personal Savior
to travel this life's highway
(this long *road* to heaven)
His yoke in me *has* made me able to *coped* with life,
And not be shaken by the things I see and hear.
Yet, I am still here giving Him praise.
I may not go to church…as often as I should.
Though long as I have breath in my body I will say," Thank you Jehovah
in Jesus name…"
Now you see how God provides through out the raging storm.
He is God of His word that will never forfeit the promised that He carry
at the cross on the hills of Calvary.
We came with a price that were purchased by God for our sins to be released;
from strongholds that had His people bound in bondaged.
We can right now give God praise forever and forevermore…
If you know that life has given you a bad deck of cards…
Try Jesus he will give you a winning deck to weep what *you* have sowed
for *others* as well as yourself…
This is what I keep in mind on a daily basic in life to *cope*: coming and going, in and
out
the revolving doors that are sat before me to choose everyday…
I just cope with it.

© 2005 Coping by Charles Jones

179